GREAT EASTERN RAILWAY
ENGINE SHEDS

EASTERN DIVISION. COLCHESTER.

Country End, looking Up.

11th May 1921. No 215.

GREAT EASTERN RAILWAY
ENGINE SHEDS

PART TWO

Ipswich and Cambridge
Locomotive Districts

BY

CHRIS HAWKINS & GEORGE REEVE

WILD SWAN PUBLICATIONS LTD.

ISBN 0 906867 48 7

FOR
RICHARD HARDY

Designed by Paul Karau
Typesetting by Berkshire Publishing Services
Printed and bound by Butler & Tanner, Frome

Published by
WILD SWAN PUBLICATIONS LTD.
1-3 Hagbourne Road, Didcot, Oxon OX11 8DP

CONTENTS

Ipswich post-nationalisation.   *H. N. James*

PREFACE

Part Two describes the remaining Great Eastern Railway Running Districts, as constituted in 1914. Part One was concerned with Stratford, Peterborough and Norwich, and this account is completed herein with Ipswich and Cambridge. As the preface to Part One noted, the Great Eastern had a perverse (and welcome) aversion to over-precise classification in these matters, and oddities are noted where appropriate (e.g. Ipswich Docks). The book was separated into two parts in order to make use of as many photographs as possible and to find room for various appendices — Raven's report, allocations, etc. The book is intended to represent the history of the various sheds throughout their existence though gaps are obvious, particularly concerning some of the smaller and more obscure sites. LNER and BR material is afforded equal significance with Great Eastern whilst diesel days and BR codings are relatively neglected. Generally the LNER/ER engine classification has been followed, confined to the main groupings.

The track plans are all based on official surveys and are reproduced to a uniform scale of approximately 2 chains to 1 inch unless otherwise stated.

ERRORS AND OMISSIONS

Comforted by the truism that books are memorable for errors more so than any revelation they might contain, it is time to record one or two bloomers in Part One. The misapplication of some direction labels on the Stratford diagram (p. 24-25) did not, it is hoped, detract too much from the intended effect, i.e. to show where the shed actually lay. More seriously, the enthusiastic description of the March barracks overlooked the somewhat unfortunate fact that this was the wrong building (!). The £1,470 mentioned on page 131 would have referred to the Enginemen's Barracks in Station Road, March, whilst the two pictures (p. 131) depict the interior of a less permanent building put up in the war for 'itinerant labourers and such' and long known as 'Belsen'. The genuine barracks provided a room and bed for each man, and as Ron Fareham points out, footplatemen would never have accepted the accommodation shown.

Peter Proud has written to point out that the Ilford 'N7' series (p. 56) is wrong, and was in fact 2600, 2221-39, not simply 2631-39. The East Anglian TPOs started in March 1929, *not* 1920 (p. 108) and on p. 195 the date is obviously wrong. 1917 should read 1927.

vi

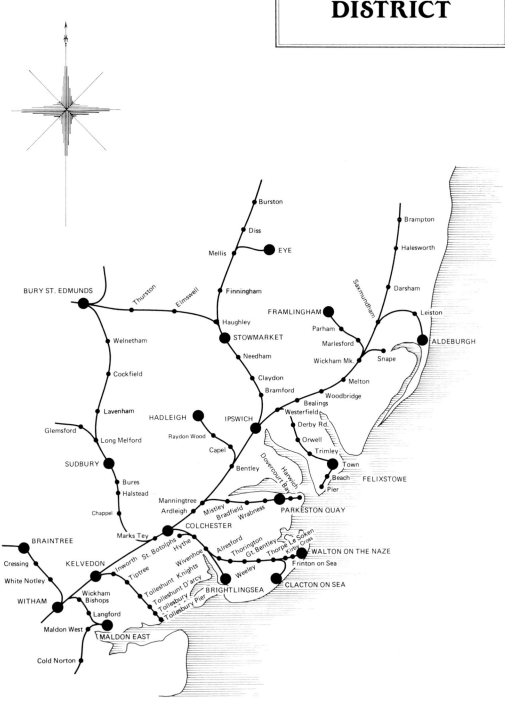

IPSWICH LOCOMOTIVE DISTRICT

Burston
Diss
EYE
Mellis
Brampton
Halesworth
Darsham
BURY ST. EDMUNDS
Thurston
Elmswell
Finningham
FRAMLINGHAM
Saxmundham
Leiston
Haughley
STOWMARKET
Parham
Welnetham
Needham
Marlesford
ALDEBURGH
Cockfield
Wickham Mk.
Snape
Claydon
Melton
Bramford
Woodbridge
Lavenham
Bealings
Glemsford
HADLEIGH
IPSWICH
Westerfield
Long Melford
Raydon Wood
Derby Rd.
Capel
Orwell
SUDBURY
Trimley
Bentley
Town
Bures
Harwich
Beach
FELIXSTOWE
Halstead
Dovercourt Bay
Pier
Chappel
Manningtree
Mistley
Bradfield
Wrabness
Ardleigh
PARKESTON QUAY
Marks Tey
COLCHESTER
BRAINTREE
St. Botolphs
Hythe
Alresford
Thorpe Le Soken
Cressing
KELVEDON
Inworth
Wivenhoe
Thorington
Gt. Bentley
Kirby Cross
WALTON ON THE NAZE
Tiptree
Tolleshunt Knights
Weeley
Frinton on Sea
White Notley
Tolleshunt D'arcy
BRIGHTLINGSEA
CLACTON ON SEA
WITHAM
Wickham Bishops
Tollesbury
Langford
Tollesbury Pier
Maldon West
MALDON EAST
Cold Norton

The street of Reverend Croft looked out over painstakingly constructed mounds and rows of coal, swelling and shrinking with the highly-tuned GER buying policy. Most of the residents were company servants and their sensibilities were suitably irrelevant.

National Railway Museum

Ipswich, placed in the period around 1900. Here are the main buildings before further accommodation was tacked onto the front to form the Ipswich 'outstation shops'. On more prosperous railways the whole site would probably have been cleared away and rebuilt by about 1880 but in such unpromising circumstances a quite excellent level of craftsmanship and skill was made possible. This situation remained so until the 1950s.

L & GRP, courtesy David & Charles

IPSWICH

The Eastern Union Railway opened its Ipswich terminus in 1846, at a semi-rural site below Stoke Hill. The Reverend S. Croft owned land nearby and lent his name to the depot, through 'Croft Street', rows of terraced houses subsequently erected at the rear of the shed. Trains from the north reversed into the terminus until a new station opened on the far side of Stoke Hill in 1860, with the original building of 1846 abandoned. At odds with the Eastern Counties with which it connected at Colchester, the EUR established more or less from the start, an engine shed, workshops and wagon/stock repair shed. The whole Croft Street site even then was regarded as relatively temporary in nature but, subject to a breathtakingly studied neglect, the original buildings remained the basis of the engine shed through to the 1950s. A two-road 'Engine House' stood adjacent to the terminus, which began from 1860 a regression to variously overgrown and neglected sidings; the main building, effectively an early 'works', comprised four roads, connected to the 'Engine House' by a turntable. Ipswich was not finally reconstructed until the early 1950s, in a fashion aimed at easy conversion to diesel traction. This came at the beginning of the 1960s but within ten years the disastrous decline in traffic levels and a complete reappraisal of working methods etc. meant that Ipswich duties could be adequately covered from a stabling/refuelling point by the station. Most of what remained was finally demolished in 1978, leaving a part only, for the CM & EE's electrification depot.

Despite the wholly inadequate conditions, staff at Ipswich coped manfully with an ever-increasing complement and, extraordinarily, the depot contrived somehow to function also as a principal repair centre. On 19th March 1849 the Eastern Union had set about a review of its works and premises, involving an exhaustive list of stations, goods sheds, residences, etc. 'Engine Sheds' existed at both extremities of the line, at Ipswich and Colchester, with workshop facilities concentrated at the former. 'Ipswich Engine Shed and Shops, Stores and Smithies' were recommended to be insured for £1,500 and, an indication of operational patterns, the coke supply was arranged for the whole line, 'one-third to be delivered at Colchester, two-thirds at Ipswich'.

As the former station faded back into the earth, various minor additions and alterations were made to the depot. The old turntable, sited inconveniently between the two buildings, rapidly became obsolescent and was at an early date repositioned at the end of lengthy, isolated sidings in the midst of the 'Croft Street' site. Its delivery was expected 'within a few days' on 18th December 1877, the cost estimated at £410, with siding and foundations expected to approximate to some £350. A simple open coal stage, of modest dimensions, appeared more or less midway between the two depot buildings.

Thus began a long and illustrious tradition of high quality craftsmanship, carried out under the most adverse conditions. Everyday servicing, examinations, etc. were essentially an outside task at Ipswich whatever the weather, for over 100 years. In the 1950s many locos were daily still oiled, etc. on 'blank' roads, i.e. without

the benefit of pits. The only real alterations came about as a result of fire damage and even then no proper expansion occurred, though some thought, at least, was given to resiting of the premises. On 27th August 1878 a meeting took place to inquire into the recent 'Fire in the Locomotive Shops, Ipswich', with the resolution 'that a Committee be held tomorrow to enquire into the circumstances'. On 8th October, following a series of pleas, the company donated £48 14s 2d 'to cover cost of workmen's tools destroyed by the fire at Ipswich'. This elicited a grateful response, the Locomotive Superintendent conveying to the directors on 5th November the men's 'gratitude for the generosity shown therein'.

On the same day, 8th October 1878, the Traffic Committee were discussing their recent inspection of the 'premises at Ipswich . . . recently destroyed by fire'. Deliberating, the officers present determined to 'get a plan . . . for their reconstruction for Locomotive purposes and also an alternative plan for altering the position more to the West.' Suitably vague, these decisions led to no more than the restoration of the building, presumably involving new roof and some attention to the walls. Even this reconstructed building proved cramped and impoverished with regard to space; a low and claustrophobic interior, the shear legs of necessity remained outside. On 5th April 1881 came the declaration: 'An additional Engine Hoist is much wanted at Ipswich' and at £170 its provision was immediately recommended.

As already intimated, no change of any great note occurred after this for very many

Coal stacks dominated the open space beyond the depot at Ipswich (a site where years before a generously laid out new shed could have been built), on a scale to suggest a strategically 'regional' stacking policy. The various piles of clinker mark the Ipswich disposal ground, and fire or smokebox debris always demanded the attendant GE wooden wheelbarrow.   *National Railway Museum*

The Ipswich turntable enjoyed a novel site, tucked away most inconveniently on a long siding, rather like the centre of a maze.

National Railway Museum

One of the original buildings at Ipswich, the two road 'Engine House' of 1846; it was used for boiler washing over many years, but was demolished (in 1939 according to local legend), leaving only the attached mess room, carpenter's shop and paint shop. Every corner at Ipswich was put to some use and the various parts and bits represent the detritus of engine and stock shopping, the typical 'back yard'.   *National Railway Museum*

Croft Street looked out over a sea of coal. Spare ground, particularly in later years when it seems the coal stocks were generally reduced, were given over to allotments for staff; this horticultural tradition evidently relieved the industrial look of the place, for Geoffrey Pember (GER *Journal* No. 34) recalls the pleasant and "comparatively 'rural'" approach to the depot "through a shrubbery with pampas grass waving in the breeze, rather than through a drab underground passage as at Stratford". P. C. Wilby has made some considered notes relating to Ipswich shed, a record of men who worked there in the earliest years of this century; housing round about was very basic and allotments were no pastime. At Ipswich, as elsewhere, a twelve hour day, six days a week, was *de rigueur*. This was hard enough, but at Ipswich the contemporary regime made it difficult not to be seen attending at the mission hut on Sundays. Non appearance, it was felt, could mean certain difficulties for one's position at work.
National Railway Museum

It is hard to appreciate now the extraordinary range of work carried out at Ipswich, so that in a description it is hard not to return to this theme. In the 'loco' proper, only four roads were available in GE days; improvements (thought to have been made around 1911) did increase the accommodation but were less than revolutionary. Nearest the main line was the tube shop, spares store and smiths' shop, all earth floored, with the latter containing eight forges and a steam hammer. At Ipswich forgings were fabricated and repaired, whitemetalling carried out, machining, stripping of engines, and subsequent repainting. In the account of P. C. Wilby: "Next, the engine was put outside and filled with water, and along came the fireraiser to light the fire and raise steam: in attendance would be the nominated safety valve setter, who would check the operation of the safety valves and adjust them as necessary. The nominated person for this was a fellow called Arthur Percy, whose brother Jack Percy was the Mechanical Foreman from 1958 until he retired in 1966. To appreciate the work of Arthur, one has to realise that boiler safety valves were the responsibility of him alone for Ipswich Shed and every engine had to pass boiler tests laid down by the company to which Arthur was responsible; he was responsible if any safety valve was fitted and sent into service in an unsafe condition. Needless to say, none ever were; likewise the various chargehands were responsible for engine boiler, motion, wheels and bearings etc. and they were answerable to the Mechanical Foreman. Various parts required machining on a lathe, so these items would be stripped from the loco and taken over to the left-hand side of the building where lathes were provided. In here wheel sets were machined, whether the tyres, axles or motion bearings needed attention. To help the operator in his task, there was a small turntable [see plan] alongside on which the wheels were positioned for machining. In this shop, various fitting jobs were carried out. The remainder of the shop had accommodation for four locos under repair, and the remaining part comprised the running shed, where locos were given daily examination, or boiler wash-outs as they became due, usually once a week. In this part and separate were the drivers' signing-on point and fitters' cabin." *National Railway Museum*

Coal at Ipswich. Stacking of the stuff was an art-form in itself, an endless and faintly nonsensical labour. Stacks were essentially ephemeral in nature, but nevertheless constructed upon the more permanent principles of the drystone wall, the dross constrained by an outer armour of selected 'blocks'.   *National Railway Museum*

years. 'A short siding . . . in connection with the recently rebuilt sand furnace' was approved in April 1893 at a cost of £72, together with a new water crane, in its turn costing £80. Despite neglect, the depot was, nevertheless, by an early date a major maintenance and running centre with repair work at an annual rate higher even than that of Norwich, despite the latter's relatively palatial facilities. Before an LNER rundown of such work began, there were 82 'workmen' involved in locomotive repairs, representing a significant decline from 1914, the height of the shed's activity. The District Locomotive Superintendent at Ipswich then had charge of over 100 footplate crews, plus another 20 or so engaged on 'certain branches' and several outstations. The 'branches' in 1914 comprised the following, all with drivers-in-charge: Kelvedon, Witham, Maldon, Braintree, Brightlingsea, Clacton, Walton-on-Naze and Sudbury. Pumpers or 'Examiners' were based in addition at Marks Tey, Thorpe-le-Soken and Long Melford. All were administered from a busy and important 'sub-shed' at Colchester, with its own foreman and inspector. 'Parkeston and Harwich' was ruled in similar fashion whilst at Bury a fitter-in-charge was responsible for some 33 staff. There were drivers-in-charge at what might strictly be termed Ipswich outstations as follows: Felixstowe, Aldeburgh, Framlingham, Hadleigh, Eye and Stowmarket. The boiler staff at Colchester were the responsibility of the Ipswich Boiler Foreman, C. Coleman, who had nearly 30 staff at the main depot, whilst the foreman fitter alone was

'Crystal Palace' tank No. 1300 at Ipswich and more or less new on 6th September 1909.
                                                                                                                      K. Nunn/LCGB

Trams Nos. 125 and 139 on 30th April 1910. They were a feature at Ipswich, coming back from the docks at weekends for attention. Along with small tank engines, they were generally dealt with in this area at the rear of the shed. The only pit hereabouts was at the end of a short siding which terminated by the stores (see plan) – piston work and most everything else on the small tanks and trams relied on this pit, universally known, with customary inpenetrable logic, as the 'Tender Road'.
K. Nunn/LCGB

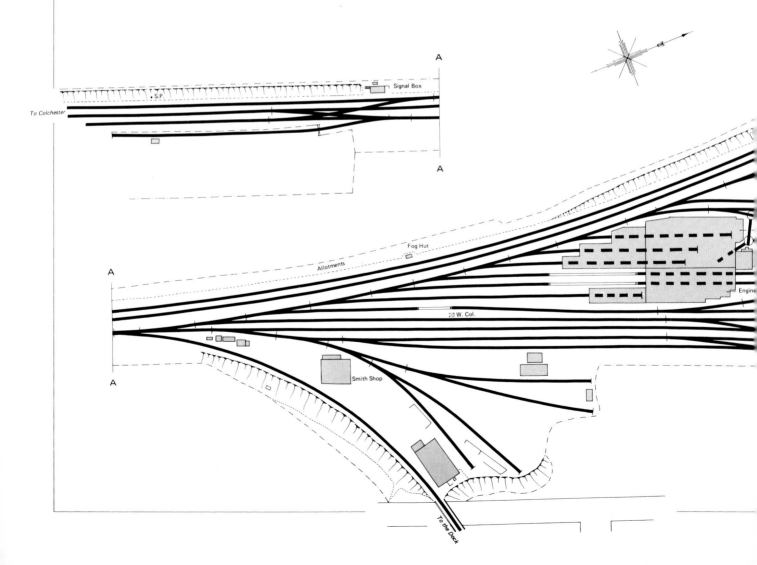

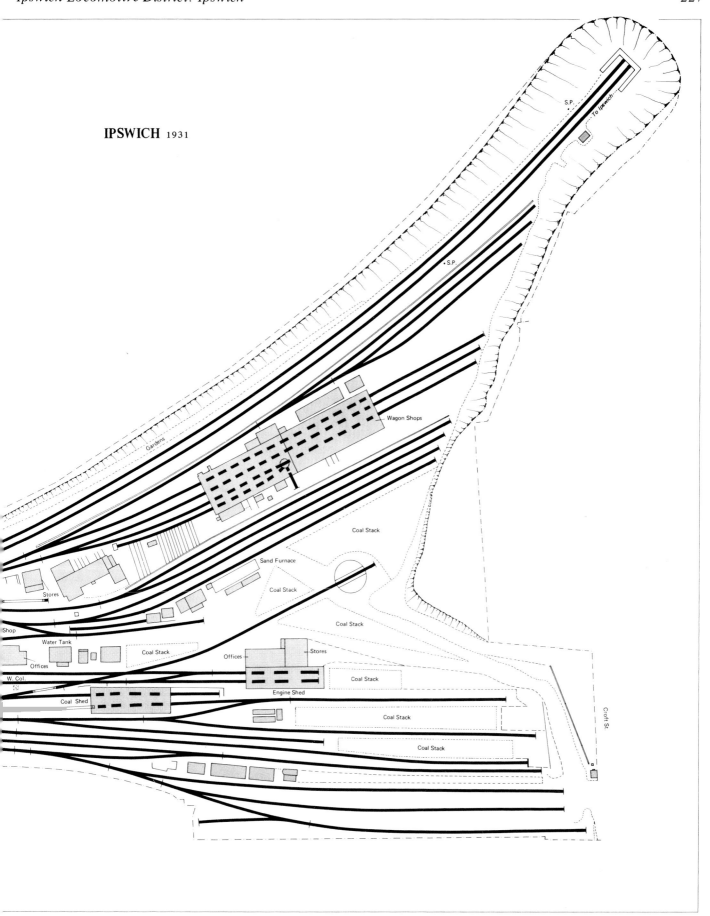

IPSWICH 1931

Oil fuelling at Ipswich. The pumps and delivery apparatus were established on the easternmost approach road, known invariably, even after the diesels arrived, as the 'Tar Road'. After the oil fuel disappeared, it was long used for 'stopped' work.   *K. Nunn/LCGB*

responsible for some 80 men. The nearby wagon works was also of some note by this time, employing 100 or so staff; a tender, for 'New Waggon Shops Ipswich' had been accepted in February 1879, at £1,487.

On the running side, Ipswich was responsible for trains of quite considerable importance, standing as it did astride the main line, with goods traffic to the docks also important. Administration of the shed at Parkeston meant Ipswich locos also worked the prestigious Harwich boat trains; Mr. G. Pember, writing in the GERS *Journal* of April 1983, points out that Ipswich involvement in trains the importance of, say, the 'Norfolk Coast Express', was, in a way, anomalous and almost certainly due to the peculiar status of Stratford. There, the most experienced men of the top link were engaged on suburban workings. Such expresses could hardly be entrusted to lower links and so Ipswich acquired the job, 'roughly half way between London and Cromer, on alternate days'.

The paucity of space at Ipswich remained, however, little short of a scandal, relieved only, it would seem, by the early establishment and development of a turntable, with pits, sidings, office, etc. adjacent to the main station. Such indigence was matched by the squalor of everyday, human facilities, an insufficiency which did not only afflict Ipswich. Toilets, etc. at some engine sheds in the 1960s could reasonably be described as horrific. The facilities at Ipswich, according to Mr. Wilfred Brown, comprised a single flush for six separate toilets, a miserly but very cleanly kept provision in

any event completely exposed to the weather. There was nowhere to wash or eat and only the most primitive first aid. Hospital cases went in a wheeled litter, really serious accidents warranting a taxi.

Men showed less inclination to accept the worst privations in the period following the Great War, when the GER, for instance, hurriedly and belatedly set about improving coaling facilities at a number of its major depots. 5th July 1917: 'Proposed shelter for coalmen, Ipswich . . . is done in the open at all hours of the day and night, the men engaged in the work being exposed to all weathers. The question has also come before the Conciliation Board'. A corrugated iron roof was then approved at a cost of £410. As we have seen, the sidings, formerly the terminus approach, etc., had perforce soon been given over to loco use, remaining so until the end of steam, and by May 1918, with war traffic at its height, some provision to ease the resulting complications was discussed: 'To facilitate the coaling of engines in the loco sidings at Halifax Junction and to get them to the engine shed afterwards, a new connection should be laid in (£113)'. On 6th November 1919 it was agreed that £422 should be expended in order to lengthen the engine pit outside the boiler shop at Ipswich by 66 yards and the following March came the startling realisation, that 'owing to lack of covered accommodation at . . . Ipswich . . . repairs are not carried out as quickly as desirable.' £1,335 was agreed for Ipswich, concluding with the statement 'The war and other reasons have caused our engine repairs to

get behind to the detriment of our traffic workings'. This sum was additional to £430 noted under 'works complete' in June 1911, for 'improvement of workshops and provision of machinery'.

Repair work began to be removed from Ipswich, transferred to Stratford, etc. from about the mid-'twenties. Raven, in 1923, reported to his new directors that 'I would certainly recommend that the building of stock should not be undertaken at Stratford in the future' and that 'I would suggest that means be taken early to close down the subsidiary workshops which are in no way well equipped and concentrate all the repairs at Stratford which should be more satisfactory and economical'. The main building at Ipswich was by this time divided more or less into three, with two roads on the east side devoted to an 'engine shed' for examination and repair work, etc., an expanded 'fitting shop' occupying the middle space, with smithy shops, etc. on the west side. This 'works' was so ill-equipped that it was easily transformed into a conventional 'repair shop', still overcrowded despite a greatly reduced level of staff and activity.

Mr. Percy Wilby has written a comprehensive description of Ipswich depot more or less at the end of the LNER era, from the entrance in Croft Street, opposite the 'EUR' pub to the internal arrangements of the shed itself. The depot was approached across waste ground, through a sleeper fence and railwaymen's allotments, the first building encountered being the remains of the early two-road 'Engine House'. It had been demolished, apparently as

Ipswich on 8th February 1946. Wartime had seen 2−8−0s and the big LNER moguls but freight work out of Ipswich remained largely 0−6−0 work. *The Railway Observer* lists the December 1932 allocation thus, making no mention of tram engines: B12: 8509/15/9/25/9/35/9/44/62-4/ 76/7/80. B17: 2806/7/20/1/5. D13: 7700/41/4. D15: 8025/37, 8799, 8803/7/14/5/7/9/20/39/41/2/4/55/69/75/85/8/92. D16: 8780. E4: 7408/ 10/4/34/66/7/70/8/81/98, 7504. F3: 8040-3/64-6/8-73/5/7. J15: 7525/38/9/41/5/56/9/69/96, 7641/89. 7815/23/41/66/73/80/91, 7914/33/4/ 6/7/9-41, 07039. J17: 8214. J39: 2771. J65: 7152/6/7, 7247. J66: 7292/5/6, 7315/22/3. J67: 7013/6, 7333/6. *Collection J. Hooper*

Percy Wilby's 'not very imposing' shed. Imposing it certainly wasn't, a hotch-potch of corrugated iron put up around the drop pit and constituting the Ipswich 'fitting shop', 5th February 1946.
British Railways

A rural railway the Great Eastern may have been, but the sheds could be as darkly brooding as any coalfield or industrial centre. Photographed from the top of the water softener, amongst all these varied buildings a total of only *eleven* engines could be worked on under cover.

British Railways

8th February 1946, illustrating the proximity of the wagon shops and the clutter of vehicles and stock. The water softener was almost the only modern structure on the whole site and the base provided a useful storeroom: "Inside the 100 foot tower were accommodated oil for locos and tools for each engine, which drivers were issued before starting out on a journey. The tools would consist of a bucket, coal hammer, oil lamps for the marking of the train, including a rear lamp, and a gauge lamp, for illuminating the gauges in the cab, a shovel and fire irons consisting of a pricker and slice, and, most important, an oil-can and cloth. The keener fellows used to have tins for paraffin for rubbing on the bright metals, also abrasive cloth and tallow, but these were not official issue. The preparation of a loco as far as the crew was concerned was for the firemen to check the coal and water carried, the state of the fire, the cleanliness of the fire tubes and footplate."   *British Railways*

early as 1939, leaving only the attached carpenters' shop, mess, brake store, etc. It had a brick floor, ordered 'to be broken up' in the BR rebuilding. With commendable understatement, Mr. Wilby describes the main shed as 'not very imposing' – by this period a mixture of brick, wood and corrugated sheeting. It incorporated tube shop, smiths, etc., the latter possessing eight forges and a steam hammer. This last item still lies buried beneath the original earth floor.

The rebuilding of Ipswich finally took place in 1953, a protracted saga, the beginnings of which can be traced back to the 1920s. A quite unacceptable situation had long existed at Ipswich (as we have seen) but apart from the sustained rundown of the major repair work, no remedial measures were put in hand. On 24th March 1927 the Divisional General Manager, having gained approval for engine pit extensions costing £360 was moved to warn that the depot 'was in need of urgent replacement and that it would not be too far into the future when a scheme for its general improvement will be required to be taken into consideration'. Thereafter Ipswich absents itself from the record, until January 1934 when a water softener was authorised, part of the GE programme, with a capacity of 105 million gallons p.a., estimated to cost in all over £9,000. The tender for the plant itself, without, of course, the extensive piping, pumps, etc. was accepted on 31st May, the Kennicott Water Softener Co. being successful with a 20,000 gallons per hour machine, at £1,717 15s 0d. Around the same time '2 Spray Cleaning

The original water tower at Ipswich was dwarfed in comparison and belonged firmly in a much earlier age, remnants of which littered the site at Ipswich. Some long forgotten rails lie at right angles to the shed roads and the verandahed window is a pleasing survivor.   *British Railways*

Machines for cleaning engines' were authorised, at a cost of £244. The softener, etc. had been part of an area scheme and the 'thirties were drawing to a close when firm proposals were at last available for rebuilding the shed itself. On 23rd June 1938 the LNER Locomotive Committee commended to the Board 'improvements at the locomotive depot at Halifax Junction' which, together with various minor alterations in the London area, totalled £76,241. On 24th November a new Ransomes Rapier wheeldrop was approved, at a cost of £1,393.

Events proceeded only slowly and by the outbreak of war it appears that, although the wheeldrop had been brought into use, little or nothing (apart from the demolition) of the two-road shed had been accomplished. On 25th July 1940 the Locomotive Committee were forcefully reminded by an increasingly desperate Loco Superintendent that the existing 45 ft 9 in 'table was in an extremely poor state. Moreover, a new 70 ft unit, purchased locally from Ransomes Rapier for over £4,500, had been delivered and was 'lying idle and starting to deteriorate'. He begged leave to authorise its immediate installation but on the same day the verdict came: 'Improvements at loco depot, Ipswich, deferred for duration of hostilities'. They had at last matured into definite plans, etc. by February 1939 but all of the welcome new features, 70 ft 'table,

The last F3 2–4–2T, No. 67127, saw out its days as the Ipswich wagon works stationary boiler. This photograph was taken on 1st February 1953. All types of work went on at Ipswich and, as well as the wagon and loco people, there was even a bus garage. It stood at the corner of Croft Street and Wherstead Road and housed buses plying between the station and Shotley Pier. The vehicles were built at Stratford and, despite a spartan interior, were considered a great advance upon the old carriers' carts or Shanks's pony. The garage became a maintenance depot for railway-owned vehicles, moving to the former examination shed in 1964.   *H. N. James*

The Ipswich coal shelter, a tribute to simplicity, if not much else.   *British Railways*

The remodelling of Ipswich depot got underway during 1953, a start being made with the administrative block. Beyond is the concrete frame (four pillars and lintels) of the 'Engine Examination and Lubrication Shed' and the first uprights of the new depot building.   *H. N. James*

Some weeks have passed since the occasion of the photograph above. The work progressed steadily enough through the summer of 1953 and this photograph of 16th July illustrates how the job proceeded, as it were, westwards, and how, as far as possible, daily activity was allowed to continue.   *British Railways*

The main shed itself was the last of the buildings to be completed and all the 'elliptical spans' are in place here, by early October 1953. It makes a useful comparison with the earlier view on page 233, and illustrates the process of demolition as much as construction. *British Railways*

Wet ash pit nearing completion on 16th July 1953. As the text outlines, these were a peculiarly LNER concept, a device carried over into BR days, presumably through the experiences of the Eastern Region Engineer. Ipswich was also equipped with a sand delivery system, through flexible hosing; the ash pit was cleaned out using a mechanical digger (these had a long and involved career at Ipswich, put to many uses), the sections of iron grille being removable. *British Railways*

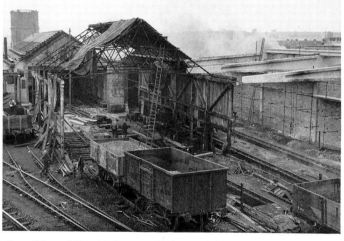

Inside what was to become the 'Engine Repair Bay', roads 1 and 2 separated from the 'running' roads 3-6 by a brick screen and enjoying the benefits of separate doors. To the left, in the retained portion of the old shed, the wheel lathe and wheel drop were to be resited. 13th January 1954. *British Railways*

Demolition of the old shops at the front of the shed, in July 1953. The original buildings lie behind and are a contrast to the simple corrugated iron on timber frame construction. The free-standing qualities of the concrete roof beams were a feature of the depot design. *British Railways*

Fabricating pits in the Repair Bay, 13th January 1954. The entire foundations were dug out, a concrete bed laid and the rail supports built up from there. *British Railways*

A minor miracle of organisation, it was nevertheless a sore trial to keep things moving at Ipswich in that winter of 1953-54. Not least amongst the problems was the increased hazard of accident, with so many men, unfamiliar with engine movements, about the site. *British Railways*

coaling plant and new concrete running shed, were once again in abeyance.

How it was at Ipswich over the following years with black-out (made 'less of an inconvenience' through continued gas lighting [!]), increased workload and reduced staff is best left to the imagination. Events were delayed, incredibly, even beyond the immediate post-war period and it was British Railways, with dieselisation as much in mind as anything, that finally rebuilt the whole decrepit affair. The reconstruction in proper Ipswich tradition was complex in itself; inevitably part of the ancient building was retained whilst, it turns out, the project was marred by tragedy. The plans were dated 29th April 1952 but do not seem to have got underway until the following year, though the rusting 70 ft turntable of 1940 had been installed 'during the war', on a site near the Wherstead Road. This had improved life somewhat but by this time it was still only possible to stable eleven engines under cover, with examination and preparation still carried out on the old 'terminus' roads. Four tender locos only were accommodated in the 'running shed', usually undergoing washout plus any other attention which could be conveniently fitted in. A track on the west side of the shed, known obscurely as 'the Tender Road', was devoted to piston work etc. on the trams (for the docks) and other small tanks. The 'Tar

Work began on the coaler toward the end of 1953 and was not fully complete until 1955. It was a remarkable exercise in concrete, owing its peculiar angles and unlikely proportions to the exceptional properties available to design in reinforced concrete. An odd system of tub loading was involved with machinery housed in the separate adjacent 'pod'. *British Railways*

Ipswich shed on 22nd April 1954.

British Railways

Road' lay on the opposite side of the yard and was a leftover from oil burning days. Coaling presented an appalling prospect, with ancient and untrustworthy caterpillar diggers expected to provide for no less than 91 locomotives.

The standard of maintenance right through to the diesel era nevertheless remained extremely high at Ipswich, due in no small part to a number of 'time-served' Ransomes Rapier men, reinforcing the LNER staff. One of the original repair bays was to remain, alongside a refurbished smith's shop, the whole constituting a modernised machine shop. The wheel drop of 1938 would be resited, along with the wheel lathe. The wholly new building was a fine up-to-date affair of six roads, built in the pre-cast concrete by now favoured on BR. In layout it was closely based on the LNER project of 1939; numbered from west to east, the first two of six roads comprised an 'engine repair bay' with the four remaining roads forming the 'running shed' proper. The building was of generous proportions allowing, on dieselisation, for servicing platforms, overhead travelling crane, etc. The roof was carried over the 'running shed' on concrete beams, cast on site in one piece. During construction, the crane jibs placing them in position dislodged one beam before it had been fastened, and it came crashing down, killing the operator.

The LNER in its latter days had conceived a liking for separate, illuminated and self-contained inspection facilities. Unknown elsewhere (it is believed), they seem to have

Smoke chutes were of fairly traditional construction, wood on a metal frame, lagged as a precaution against corrosion. These items were photographed on 15th November 1954 and would represent the last additions to the new depot.

British Railways

Ipswich (above) on 30th August 1954 and (below) on 15th November. The design, in its layout at least, had first been arrived at in 1938-39, and revised in April 1946.
British Railways

The shed in August of 1954. It was said to have been erected with diesels in mind and, indeed, it had an exceptionally modern look, recalling as few of our railway buildings did, the new modernism finding some acclaim across France and parts of Europe. Most of the concrete was cast on site during construction, including the beams, and mention is made in the text of the dislodgement of one, with fatal results. Several locomotives were also damaged in the incident, which received considerable press coverage locally; the national event, however, was the Coronation, suitably recorded in the bricks of the new building.

British Railways

30th August 1954. The examination buildings were regarded as excellent. They could be properly lit, twenty-four hours a day and were of a size allowing both efficient heat and a handy concentration of tools and equipment.   *British Railways*

appeared in response to the greater financial stringency suffered by the LNER. Lightweight covered pits were presumably cheaper than permanent brick and concrete structures. Such a separate, 'Engine Examination and Lubrication Shed' was supplied by BR at Ipswich, on the east side of the main building. A short distance to the north a new concrete coaling plant was established, a wagon tippler type with two delivery chutes and, further on, a wet ash pit. 160 ft in length, it represented another perpetuation of LNER principles – such pits allowed hot debris to be cast directly into a concrete sink of suitable depth. The immediate dowsing of such unpleasant waste was of considerable advantage but the resultant sludge required periodic excavation and transfer to wagons for ultimate disposal. It was in truth 'untidy' and suffered accordingly. As such it cannot be regarded as an unfavourable reflection on LNER practice. Its financial and commercial basis was the least enviable of the 'Big Four' and the acquisition of the Great Eastern, while it did not quite pre-empt Petains' phrase 'fusion with a corpse' was nevertheless with some degree of justification described as a 'rural millstone'.

Locomotives in the Ipswich District must have totalled a hundred or so prior to the First World War and from LNER days through to the onset of dieselisation, seventy to eighty engines were regularly based at the main shed. All manner of 0–6–0 and 2–4–2Ts came in from the sub-sheds periodically, including the trams on dock work. Throughout the years, of course, virtually all the passenger, freight and tank types were represented. The GE '1500' 4–6–0s gave way to 'B17s' and 'B1s' although goods work remained largely the preserve of 0–6–0 types, the older GE models supplemented by 'J39s' of LNER origin. Norwich and Stratford Britannia Pacifics could frequently be found at the shed; similarly Southern Region 4–6–2s during the 'loan' period of the early 1950s.

Though it remained an important maintenance centre, Ipswich ceased to head its own district around 1938 and was afterwards, throughout BR days, listed under Norwich.

The *Railway Magazine* of January 1960 reported that re-equipment had been going on at Ipswich for some time and that it was now 'the first main-line motive power depot in the country to be converted entirely from steam to diesel working for both passenger and freight services under the modernisation plan'. The article went on to note that Ipswich locomotives worked trains between Lowestoft, Yarmouth,

Ipswich and London and cross-country services to Whitemoor. Twenty-seven Type 2 diesels, BR built as well as Brush and NBL units, were said to have replaced sixty steam locomotives, whilst 'between 20 and 30' diesel shunters were also maintained. Hunslet 0–6–0s in the 11100 series had in fact arrived, mainly intended for dock work, as early as 1952. The following *Railway Magazine* comments are also of interest:

'The major part of the depot was reconstructed also in 1954 with the requirements of diesel traction in mind, which greatly facilitated the subsequent conversion to

The 'admin block', something of an improvement on the Dickensian offices scattered about the old depot. It fronted Wherstead Road near the 'Black Bridge' (visible in several of the photographs) which carried the dock line over the road. It contained enginemen's signing-on lobby and a mess with gas cooker, cupboards and sinks and even hot and cold running water. There was a store with modern racking and office, a cycle rack, oil store and first aid room underneath, whilst the top floor provided for the shed master and his staff, a lecture room, cloakroom, toilets and showers.   *British Railways*

The layout of the depot and the relation of the buildings, one to another, seen to good effect in 1956.   *Collection John Hooper*

The 'inlet road' at Ipswich, for the purposes of the servicing sequence, ran beneath the coaler, the line adjacent being the 'outlet road'. 'Examination and Lubrication' in the separate shed were generally the responsibility of the shift chargehand who then gave resulting repair jobs to the appropriate fitter or boilermaker.
                                                                                                                              British Railways

Coaling at Ipswich was revolution-ised (though over-late) with the introduction of mechanical plant. Before, it had been carried out essentially by hand, or at best using diggers and loaders. Up to the rebuilding, an RB10 diesel and a Fordson petrol tractor with bucket had been in use. Both were prey to mechanical break-down and the weather.

W. Potter

No. 61535 at the shed, on a Sunday before rebuilding of the depot. The engine, washed out and lit up and being cleaned prior to turning for a London working, masked the stationary boiler and an associated passageway, known as 'The Portable'(!). Just off to the right was a door into the list clerk's office, which led to the shedmaster, the general office and by a further passage to the office of the mechanical foreman. On the right of the group stands R. H. N. Hardy, in charge at the depot in the year prior to rebuilding. These books owe much to his reminiscence and kind advice.

H. N. James

Train passing Ipswich around 1950. The allocation that year was made up of the following: B1 4−6−0: 61052, 61053, 61054, 61055, 61058, 61059, 61201, 61252, 61253, 61254; B12 4−6−0: 61535, 61561, 61562, 61564, 61566, 61568, 61569, 61570, 61577; B17 4−6−0: 61600 *Sandringham*, 61601 *Holkham*; 61604 *Elveden*; 61618 *Wynyard Park*, 61634 *Hinchingbrooke*, 61645 *The Suffolk Regiment*, 61649 *Sheffield United*, 61668 *Bradford City*, 61669 *Barnsley*; D16 4−4−0: 62526, 62590; J39 0−6−0: 64752, 64785, 64793, 64800, 64803, 64826, 64829, 64834, 64841, 64894, 64900, 64905, 64957, 64958: J15 0−6−0: 65408, 65422, 65430, 65447, 65459, 65467; J17: 0−6−0: 65578; F6 2−4−2T: 67220, 67230, 67239; L1 2−6−4T: 67702, 67703, 67704, 67705, 67706, 67708, 67709, 67711, 67716, 67719, 67787; J65 0−6−0T: 68211; Tram J70: 68216, 68220, 68221, 68224; J67/69: 68498, 68518, 68593.
H. N. James

diesel maintenance. An unusual feature of the new building was the form of pre-stressed concrete running-shed roof-members, from each of which a cantilever portion spanned the maintenance bay before additional support was available from the more recent fitting shop partition.

'One of the most important of the recent civil engineering tasks was the removal of smoke chutes and flues and general cleaning to remove the grime deposits left by steam locomotives. Inspection pits and the shallower side pits were modified to suit the new requirements and flanked by service platforms of concrete, 4 ft 6 in above rail level. A common centre portion joining the six platform-ends forms a bridgehead and ramp leading through the partition and into the fitting shop. Thus wheeled trucks can run from the high-level platforms directly into the fitting shop to distribute and collect engine parts, filter panels, and so on. A 15 cwt hand-operated travelling crane covers all the normal lifting requirements of two repair bays at the south end of the shop.'

Thus was progress at Ipswich accelerated in the final years, the shed, remarkably, being closed down in 1968. Ten years later, much of what remained was demolished.

No. 64826, of the considerable Ipswich stud of J39 0−6−0s. There was a concentration of these engines at Ipswich, and relatively less of the GE J15 and J17 locos than were to be found at, say, Norwich.
H. N. James

Ipswich in May 1952.   *H. N. James*

Harewood House on the Ipswich turntable. The B17s had been something of a considerable advance on the GE section, and wage cuts imposed in the 'twenties were traditionally laid at their door, the LNER having to find the cash somewhere. They were in charge of much of the main line work until Britannia Pacifics arrived.   *H. N. James*

Steam at the new shed had a relatively short life, being effectively ousted by 1960. The last engine, however, was a B1 4−6−0, returning to East Anglia for night time carriage heating. In 1963 a shed turner, with a certain enthusiasm for steam, was appointed when a vision-impaired predecessor was taken off the job. A Paxman Type 1 − D8223 − in his charge had ended up in Croft Street, to some embarrassment. Departmental No. 17 (ex-61252) was employed to tow it back into the confines of the shed.   *H. N. James*

L1 No. 67703 at Ipswich. The big Thompson engines replaced many of the inumerable Ipswich passenger tanks, including 2−4−2Ts on some of the 'seaside' branch workings. One such job was the Felixstowe branch, which in the 1930s had been given over to ex-Great Central 4−4−2Ts, working out of Ipswich shed.
British Railways

The first diesels at Ipswich had been shunters for the docks (the first arrived at three o'clock in the morning) though a Drewry was later customarily put on station pilot work, D2041 highly polished. Ipswich men were trained on railcars from the 'fifties but the units were based at Norwich. The pioneer main line unit was D5502, arriving as the contractors busied themselves at the shed once more, installing walkways and ramps, strip lighting, warm air heating, compressed air points and any number of exotic services. The *Railway Magazine* concluded its 1960 account: "With the elimination of steam working, the redundant coaling plant, turntable, and water columns will be removed. On part of the site occupied by these, a locomotive washing machine will be erected. Design work on this is in hand." *W. T. Stubbs*

'B1' No. 51252 is of interest in that, along with others of the class in East Anglia, it was converted for carriage steam heating after being made surplus to normal traffic requirements. As No. 17, the 4–6–0 stayed on at Ipswich, on occasion performing various minor (and illegal) tasks around the yard.

IPSWICH STATION

The new station at Ipswich was provided with locomotive facilities almost immediately. Certainly by the end of 1862 a 45 ft turntable had been installed, on the west side of the station. There were three engine sidings in all, two with pits either side of a substantial wooden 'coke stage'. Two separate water tanks were in use and this servicing point was extended and developed over the years, providing immense relief at the shed proper. On 4th February 1863 the Locomotive Committee noted that 'Express Trains now run through from Norwich and it is necessary to erect two Water Cranes at the Ipswich New Station, one on the Up and the other on the Down Line'. In 1881 engine pits were recommended in the 'Platform road' at the station, 'at each end, with a gas lamp on each'. The cost was estimated at £130.

At the end of 1912 a new siding was authorised for the turntable (which in contrast to the example at the shed itself, had been enlarged to 55 ft), 'to enable engines to work to and from the turntable without running past a fixed signal'. Fuel tanks, sidings, etc. have since been built over the site where now, an indication of the collapse in traffic levels since steam days, a handful of diesels stable between duties.

IPSWICH DOCKS

The major part of the extensive rail network threading the docks at Ipswich lay on the north side of the River Orwell, a considerable distance from the main shed. Much of the traffic by necessity crossed roads, public and otherwise, and the Great Eastern 'tram' locos could ever be found there. A 'Tramway along-side the Docks' was an early development, ordered 'to be repaired', for instance, in September 1863. A 'coke stage' was also provided from about this time but it was not until the 1890s that a proper shed was erected; on 29th April 1891 £110 was authorised for the 'Ipswich Tram Small Engine Shed and Pit'. It does not seem to have been listed along with the other 'outstations'. The single road shed, its method of construction poorly known, stood at the end of the main dock line complex, opposite the grain shed, between Commercial Road and the River Orwell. It could accommodate 'a pair of trams', with a coal stage 30 ft by 10 ft outside, along with a water column.

The trams seem finally to have succumbed in the face of dieselisation, a notable forerunner being Hunslet 0–6–0 No. 11111. Steam locos other than trams had found employment over the years, however, on quite a regular basis. At heavy periods or when trams were unserviceable, conventional 0–6–0Ts would appear, modified to 0–4–2 with removal of the rear coupling rod. Even 0–6–0 tender locos could turn up, so transformed. The shed apparently closed on full dieselisation of the dock shunting, no later presumably than about 1954-55. The *Railway Observer* lists 'Ipswich Docks' on 2nd October 1954 as having '2 J70s, 1 D.M. 0–4–0 (at 32B Ipswich at weekends)'.

The 'Tram Shed' was a quarter of a mile or so walk away, down Wherstead Road, and a regular man would be sent 'down the tram' every day. It was quite an onerous duty at one time, with night-time coaling, washing out and firebox cleaning. The station site was, of course, of more importance to the working of the passenger service at least, and enjoyed the presence of a foreman in summer (and all the time during the Second World War). The trams handled up to sixty wagons and the diesel successors operated (officially) under similar legal constraints. The 0–4–0 Hunslets, Nos. D2950-52, had a notice, in a specially constructed framing, in the cab, reminding the crew that the engine must not frighten horses, emit smoke or exceed 12 mph. Latterly a Swindon-built 03 shunter has been sufficient for the traffic, but the little shed which, despite records to the contrary, seems unlikely to have ever had room for more than a single tram, was put out of use on the end of steam. *Dr. I. C. Allen*

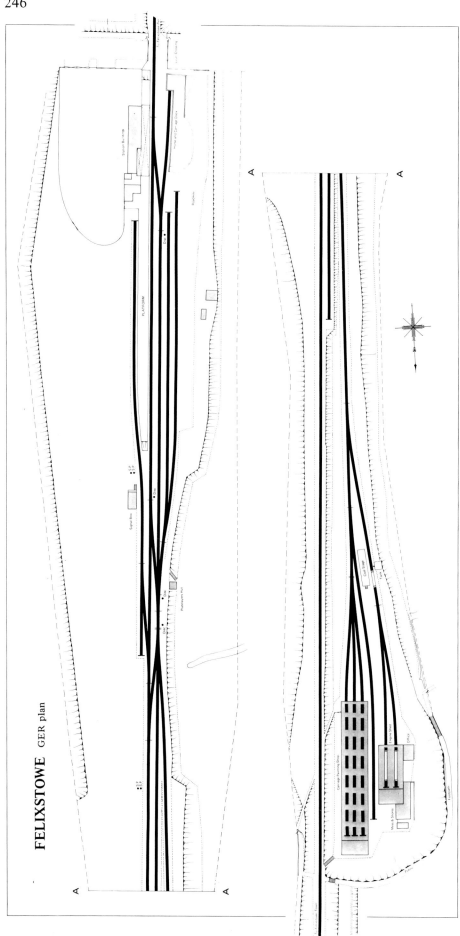

FELIXSTOWE GER plan

FELIXSTOWE

Felixstowe has an interesting if slightly contentious history, as convoluted as any of the GER's affairs. The line originally belonged to an independent concern, opened throughout in May 1877, a brief period of more or less independent operation ensuing until the latter part of 1879, when the GER finally assumed control. On 2nd December 1879 the Traffic Committee reviewed a list of material, equipment etc. 'to be taken over by this company'.

The Felixstowe company, which among other items owned three locomotives, 2–4–0Ts *Orwell, Tomline* and *Felixstowe*, erected two buildings (near to what became Felixstowe Beach station) for the maintenance of their locomotives and rolling stock, the 'engine house' subsequently forming the GE depot and the carriage shed coming to notice in latter years as a curious 'outstation' of the great Works at Stratford. The latter remained in place, put to no particularly obvious use until the 1890s, when Holden acquired it as some small recompense for the lack of carriage facilities at Stratford. The *Great Eastern Railway Magazine* of January 1911 describes it in the following fashion:

> 'The Felixstowe paint shop is used to relieve the carriage paint shops at Stratford; and during the course of a year about 200 carriages are painted there. It was originally the engine depot of the Felixstowe Railway Company; and has been used for its present purpose since January 1894.'

The magazine is surely in error somewhere here: the shed, with coal stage, water tank etc. had stood, separate from the much larger 'paint shop' since at least 1879, the two remaining unaltered well past the turn of the century. Fuelling the confusion are GER Minutes which, about the time of Holden's sequestration of the 'paint shop', seem almost to imply that the engine shed was out of use. This again must be unlikely, in view of the length of the branch, its importance, the GE's propensity for such establishments etc. 'One engine' was allocated in 1890.

Ipswich was, of course, the 'parent' shed and by 1914 the District Locomotive Superintendent there was in charge, through an assistant and a foreman, of a dozen or so men at Felixstowe, most of them acting drivers or firemen. The depot was run by a 'driver in charge' and no fitters, cleaners etc. were based there, all repairs and washouts being carried out at Ipswich. A new main station, Felixstowe Town, opened in 1898, the spur to Beach and Pier closing and a new one, involving reversal at the new station, took its place. The main development of Felixstowe as a holiday town etc. followed this. Through running to London necessitated a turntable and suitable provision was made at the new station. Referred to usually as simply 'Felixstowe', the shed commonly by now had two or three locos. In 1931, for instance, a pair of 'F3' 2–4–2Ts formed the complement and by 1935/36 a trio of ex-GC 'C14' 4–4–2Ts, 'changing frequently,' operated from the shed, outbased from Ipswich. Felixstowe, with a history that can only be described

as imperfectly known, underwent the uncharted decline and eventual disappearance common to other former GER sheds. The yard (the paint shop having 'burnt down' some years previously) was certainly in use throughout most of the 1930s, visiting goods and passenger engines making use of the ample coal stock. It is not clear if the shed building was still standing at this time but by 1950 it was no longer in use and 'Felixstowe' referred to the servicing area established on the north side of Town station.

There were two sets of men, 'who lived in the Tank House and never spoke', in charge of an 'L1' 2-6-4T, usually No. 67719. The principal branch type by this period, it was engaged all day on trips to and from Ipswich. Ipswich was responsible for all the extra work, summer passenger trains, etc. and also the 6 o'clock 'Felixstowe Goods', shunting all the yards and worked, again, by an 'L1'. A 50 ft turntable had long been provided at Town station and in October 1936 as part of 'Government Assistance Work', £126,177 was made available for the 'Modernisation of the Felixstowe Branch'. The Locomotive Committee portion was determined at £2,435, translated the following year into a 60 ft articulated turntable, the tender of £1,637 7s 6d being accepted from Cowans Sheldon on 22nd June 1937. A pit, water column and additional siding were also provided, eventually, it is assumed, allowing the abandonment of the old 'Beach' depot. By the early 1950s it is not even wholly clear whether 'a depot' was officially considered to exist at all. By 1957 only a pit and siding remained, the last trace of the old two road shed being simply a pair of tracks in what was formerly the yard.

Photographs of the engine shed at Felixstowe are not (so far at least) available. There is, however, a considerable compensation in these two records of the Felixstowe Town turntable. It served visiting locos; holiday traffic and goods come immediately to mind but for years the basic service was worked by tanks out of Ipswich. 2-4-2Ts worked the branch for years, followed by C14 4-4-2Ts, and L1s were latterly prominent. Most of the considerable Ipswich stud could be found on the work. 'Felixstowe' was reported closed in 1959 'with introduction of new diesel services on 5th January'. This would apply to the branch services but the Town turntable is likely to have remained in use or at least available for use into the following year.

National Railway Museum

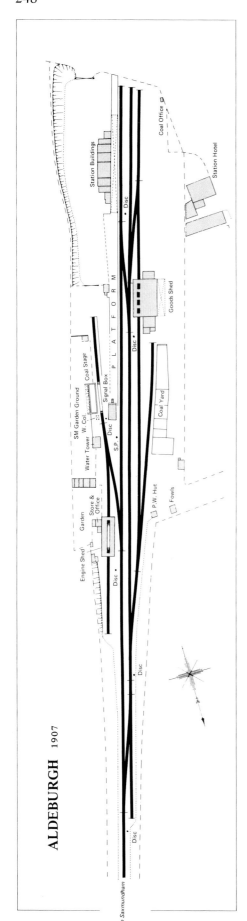

ALDEBURGH 1907

Aldeburgh on 10th October 1951. The shed has obvious affinities with other early buildings — Ongar, Framlingham and others.   *D. Clayton*

ALDEBURGH

The shed at Aldeburgh is considered to have opened, if not with the branch itself in 1860, then at some time very shortly afterwards. Certainly it had obvious affinities with other small brick engine sheds of the period — in the first years a tiny 'turnplate' and short stub siding, with crane, was provided for coaling purposes. There was never more than a single tank locomotive at Aldeburgh, worked throughout the day by only two crews; a driver in charge oversaw the general work of the shed, accompanied (in 1914) by an acting driver and two acting firemen. Coaling, as at many of these small GE establishments, was at night, a lonely task usually entrusted to a cleaner.

2–4–2Ts of various classes came to predominate on the branch passenger workings, ('F7s', GE 'Y65s' appeared more or less new around 1909) changing weekly and supplemented only by 0–6–0s on goods. 'J15s' were most commonly used, but by BR days an Ipswich 'J17' was making regular appearances, the job 'on bonus' to encourage a speedy completion. 'F3' tanks were in almost exclusive charge throughout the 1930s with 'F6s' more usual in the early 'fifties. Canon C. S. Bayes recorded the following in LNER days, information first published in the GER Society *Journal*:

16th June 1932 – 'F3' 2–4–2T No. 8075
7th November 1933 – 'F3' 2–4–2T No. 8077
[an ex-GNR 'C12' 4–4–2T was also active around this time, at least through July and August of 1933]
20th June 1935 – 'F3' 2–4–2T No. 8073
8th November 1935 – 'F3' 2–4–2T No. 8073
18th June 1936 – 'F3' 2–4–2T No. 8071
16th June 1937 – 'F3' 2–4–2T No. 8043
17th June 1937 – 'F3' 2–4–2T No. 8065
14th June 1938 – 'F1' 2–4–2T No. 5727

F3 No. 8073 at Aldeburgh on 28th April 1928. This engine appeared with some regularity on the branch and figures repeatedly in the text below. 0–4–4Ts were used in the early years and there is a record of one, Adams E10 No. 97, suffering a mishap on a branch train at Leiston, on 30th August 1882.   *W. Potter*

No. 8073 was also at the shed in mid-June 1937. The prototype Ivatt 2–6–2T No. 41200 came to Ipswich and the Aldeburgh branch in the summer of 1949 bearing the letters 'LMS' on the bunker. It had gone into service (as 1200) at Bangor in February 1947, rapidly becoming 'immensely popular'. This large and disturbing machine, however, appalled and intimidated the regular Aldeburgh driver who endlessly and doggedly reported it unfit for service — it languished often at Ipswich shed, the staff a trifle bemused but it returned for a further summer in 1950. Maybe the engine's reception was owed overmuch to the appelation 'LMS' — though certainly the high bunker would have proved a most unwelcome prospect at the primitive Aldeburgh coal stage.

DMU services began in June 1956 but the shed had reportedly gone out of use before this, closing, 'by April', the previous year.

The familiar 8073 on 17th May 1937.   *W. A. Camwell*

Aldeburgh, 9th October 1951. About this time the branch was host (in summer) to an Ivatt 2MT 2−6−2T, No. 41200. Driver Runnacles was in charge, having worked most of his life at Aldeburgh, and disliked the new tank as much as anybody, but it was difficult to send it away. The story runs that the BR chief (or at least a Board member) enjoyed a prominent membership of a local golfing club. The usual old 2−4−2T stalled one day and had to be assisted by an Ipswich light engine; the ensuing pyrotechnics unfortunately put the links to the flame. Imperiously, and with chilling speed, orders came for a better engine. No one in the chain of command dared arrange anything which could possibly be construed as inadequate and Ipswich got BR's *newest* engine − 41200 from a rather miffed Bangor. The engine came down in summertime for a few years around 1949-1951 and, as the text relates, every excuse was found to fail it. The Bangor shed plate until recently adorned a house at Thorpeness.

D. Clayton

FRAMLINGHAM 1908

91 M.P.

FRAMLINGHAM

Framlingham bore many similarities to Aldeburgh. The line, completed in 1859, was roughly contemporaneous, whilst the sheds, built to branch line standards then current, were virtually indistinguishable. Framlingham, like Aldeburgh, is assumed to have opened with the line. Again, as on the Aldeburgh line, 2–4–2Ts (of class 'F3') sufficed over very many years, outbased from Ipswich and worked by a similar complement, a driver in charge, an acting driver and two acting firemen. 'F6s' were on passenger work in the last years, around 1950/52, replacing the 'F3' tanks of the 1930s. Coaling at Framlingham was from an open platform, less substantial than the Aldeburgh example and until at least the 1880s Framlingham as well had possessed a small 'turnplate' and stub siding. The Framlingham passenger service ended in November 1952, except for school specials etc. and the shed was no longer needed.

Bottom right: Framlingham in 1951. By these latter years (certainly from the late 'forties) the shed was unused, unless it be for a severe snowstorm, the engine backing to the coal stage and staying there. The water tank bore the inscription 'Garrets, Leiston, 1859', so fixing its construction to the line's opening. As at most of these small sheds, coaling was at night; they were traditionally unsettling places, wherever one went (Swanage on the Southern, for instance, adjoined a graveyard, and Staines on the GWR was regarded as particularly creepy) such that one Framlingham man, sent 'over the edge' had to be medically committed.

Dr. I. C. Allen

No. 8068 at Framlingham on 29th March 1937. Other 2−4−2Ts noted over the years included 8064 on 16th June 1932 and 17th June 1935, 8077 on 14th June 1937 and 67239 on 17th August 1951.

W. A. Camwell

Hadleigh, a town, it seems, which existed for malt and little else.

Collection W. A. Camwell

There is an almost unreal quality to these photographs, which reveal Hadleigh to have been a thriving agricultural centre. The industry is notorious for its cyclical rounds of prosperity and bust and East Anglia has suffered a number of agricultural depressions. The heavily-laden wagon to the left is just the type which occupied Johnson in 1873 and over fifty or so years the constant business of shunting, together with the passenger service, must have kept a tank engine busily occupied.

Collection W. A. Camwell

HADLEIGH

The branch from Bentley to a terminus amid mills and malthouses at Hadleigh opened in 1847. The shed, a minute and archaic wooden structure dwarfed by its own immense coal stack, appears to have opened at the same time. Certainly it had been long in use by 1873. Traffic from Hadleigh was overwhelmingly agricultural in nature (though domestic coal came in) and the little shed lay before a complex of maltings. They had grown up around the terminus leaving the shed somewhat awkwardly sited, such to prompt a discussion, at least of its possible resiting. The proposed remedy was pure Great Eastern:

'21st May 1873. Hadleigh Engine Shed — Proposed Removal to Another Site — This shed has again sustained considerable damage by its door jambs being struck by

a truck when passing through it laden with coke. Mr. Johnson states that the traffic to and from 3 maltings all passes through the shed which is 40 feet long and only 9 feet wide so that any improperly loaded truck is almost sure to strike the door, he suggests that the shed be moved and put up on a vacant place near to the water tank close by. The cost of building a New Engine Shed together with the laying in of a New Siding thereto would be £337.

Resolved — that the Engineer ascertain if the doorway can be enlarged so as to save the expense of removing the shed'.

Later, on 18th June, the costs were compared:

'New Engine Shed and Sidings £337
Repairs to present Shed £ 55 '

The latter course was inevitably chosen and (following a lapse, of course, of several further years) steps were taken to remedy the access

problem. Until at least the early 1880s a wagon 'table had lain outside the shed's north entrance, a long siding leading off it to the maltings. This was removed to the adjacent siding so that although trucks still required to cross the shed road, it was not necessary to shunt them through the building itself. Thus were Johnson's door jambs preserved.

The 'water tank close by', to which the shed would have been 'removed', stood some distance to the south, where the sidings etc. narrowed to the branch itself. There was also a well and pump etc. but in any case, apart from the damaged shed, the tank itself was in pretty poor condition — it was timber built and only a few years after the proposed move it was described as 'much decayed and requires to be renewed'. In December 1877 a tender for its replacement was accepted, that of Pearson and Knowles Coal and Iron Company, £37 and a delivery time of six weeks.

The Eastern Union Railway initially used its minute 2—2—0T No. 28, *Ariels Girdle* of 1851 on the branch which may account for the narrow dimensions of the shed. Beyond the building and its groaning coal stage is, clearly visible, the Maltings track, and the site of the original wagon turntable. Before its removal to the adjacent road, it is hard to imagine how the engine was ever properly stabled. *Collection W. A. Camwell*

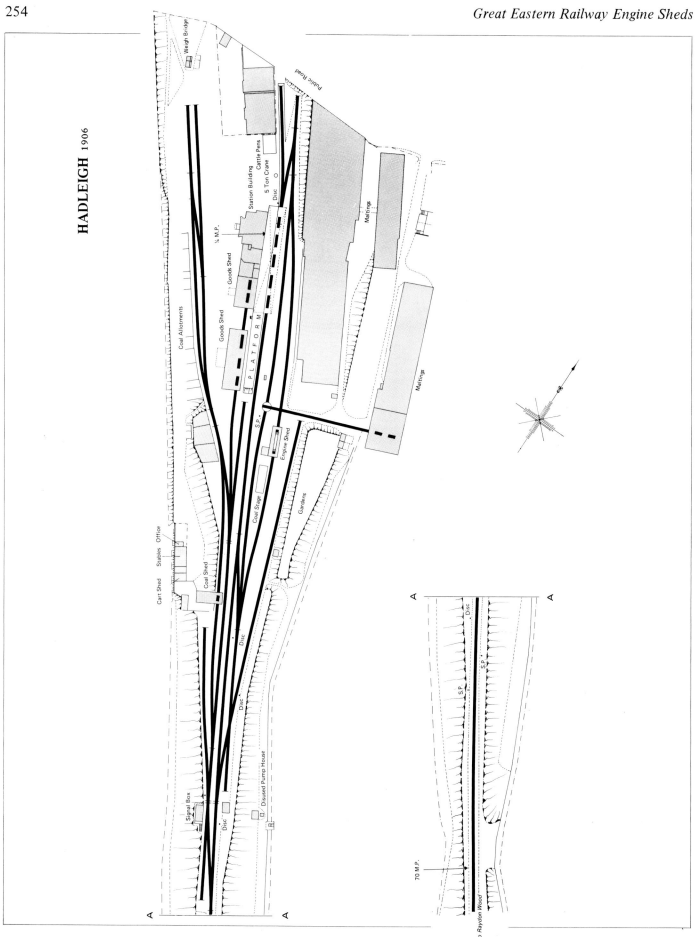

HADLEIGH 1906

Weigh Bridge

Public Road

Station Building

Cattle Pens

5 Ton Crane

Disc

¼ M.P.

Goods Shed

Goods Shed

PLATFORM

Coal Allotments

Maltings

Maltings

S.P.

Engine Shed

Coal Stage

Gardens

Cart Shed

Stables

Office

Coal Shed

Disc

Disc

Disused Pump House

Signal Box

Disc

A

A

A

A

Disc

S.P.

S.P.

70 M.P.

To Raydon Wood

A single locomotive sufficed at Hadleigh, crewed in standard fashion by a pair of acting firemen and an acting driver, under a driver in charge. The locomotive was exchanged for a fresh example from Ipswich at the appropriate interval; for many years this appears to have been a 2–4–2T withdrawn on cessation of the passenger service in 1932. The shed then closed but there was a regular goods, until the mid-1960s worked by an Ipswich engine which shunted 'as necessary'. By about 1950 the 'Hadleigh Goods' was worked 'on bonus' often with a 'J17'. Despite its light construction and the years of damage from negligently loaded wagons, the shed had still stood as late as 1924. It could not have long survived closure in 1932, H. D. Bowtell reporting in the *Railway Observer* of 1937 that 'the loco shed here is now closed and demolished'.

Hadleigh on 29th March 1937. Only the brick lean-to (or could the shed itself be more accurately described as the lean-to?) and pit remained, with traffic levels severely reduced.   *W. A. Camwell*

The Hadleigh wagon 'table. There was a daily goods for years after passenger closure; Ipswich F4 No. 7218 had been one of the last engines to work the line (it was on branch working on 19th June 1931) and an 'F7' seen at Ipswich, No. 8310, is thought to have also taken a hand on the job.   *L & GRP, courtesy David & Charles*

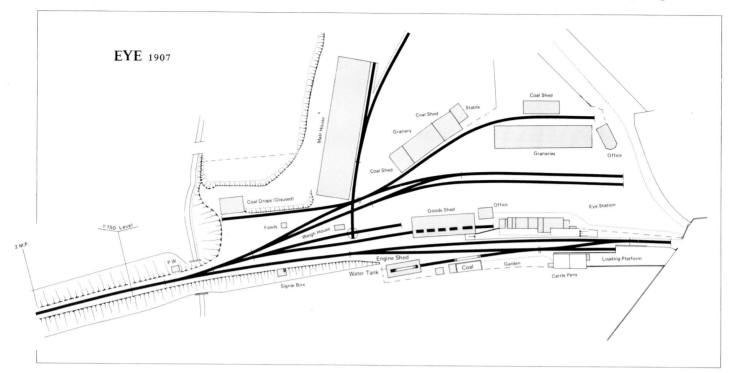

EYE 1907

EYE

The Mellis and Eye Railway opened after a prolonged altercation with the GER in April 1867. The line, ostensibly independent, was nevertheless worked by the Great Eastern with effective control exercised from the first by the larger company. It officially absorbed the Mellis and Eye in 1898.

The Great Eastern, not then responsible for finance, took great care to see everything ordered to the highest possible standard, its strictures conveniently revealing some of the earliest details of the shed. On 28th March 1866 the whole project came before the Traffic Committee with a number of suggestions from Sinclair regarding the proposed contract for the line. He urged: 'Shed Room and conveniences for housing, washing and coking an Engine should be provided in the first instance together with a small Passenger and Goods Shed as well as space for depositing Coals and standing room for a moderate quantity of Trucks'.

A Great Eastern officer, a Mr. Davis, inspected the completed line in February 1867, seeming generally impressed. He reported: 'The Engine Shed is 47' 6" x 17' 4" to stand One Engine, the Tank is of Wood and will hold about 2,000 Gallons and Water which has to be pumped by hand a tedious and expensive operation – I consider a small Donkey Engine should be provided.' The shed was thus in use from the very first, the GE outbasing an engine from Ipswich. An early insight into the latter is possible through a minute of 18th August 1868; the Locomotive Superintendent had submitted a report on the working of 'the Mellis and Eye Branch' using 'the Cambridge Engine and Gooch's small Tank Engine'. The former was a railmotor contraption, a lightweight

Remains of Eye shed on 29th March 1937. Staff here had been reduced to two only from 1921, with Nos. 7153, 7155, 7157, 7247, 7250, 7253 and 7254 amongst the engines used in the last years.
W. A. Camwell

'steam carriage' named *Cambridge* and originating with the ECR in 1849. The latter machine appears to have been a 2–2–2WT which had worked on the North Woolwich line in 1868. The Superintendent's report makes reference to it as follows:

'No. 9 Engine appears to be of the size and capacity best suited for the working of the Branch. Recommend . . . that the testing of the working of Branch Lines with light engines to continue, and when the result is obtained, such Engines as are found most suitable should be exclusively employed.'

These early inhabitants of Eye shed seem to have given way very shortly to more conven-

tional locos. Mr. P. Paye has written a history of the line (Oakwood Press 1980) and relates that from the mid-1870s 0–4–2Ts were at work followed from the 1890s by 'E22' (later 'J65') 0–6–0Ts. They held more or less exclusive sway until the withdrawal of passenger services in 1931. Mr. Paye has ascertained that the procedure at Eye was to change locomotives on Mondays, enabling the relieved engine to return to Ipswich for repairs; its replacement would then be at work for two or three weeks, with necessary attention, washout, etc. carried out on Sundays by a senior fireman on overtime. Eye was a typical 'outstation' in 1914 with four staff – the same number as Hadleigh,

Framlingham, etc. — two acting firemen and an acting driver under a driver-in-charge. In the early years two small wooden lean-tos stood against the shed but these had disappeared prior to closure. A mess also existed under the water tank, which fed a column via the locomotive's water raising cock.

The passenger service was withdrawn in February 1931; the brick shed was then promptly closed, and partly demolished.

STOWMARKET

There was a 'driver in charge' at Stowmarket in late GE days, accompanied by a further driver and a pair of acting firemen. A wide range of agricultural industries was centred on the town and the yards and sidings were surprisingly complex; in keeping with its rural origins, shunting at Stowmarket prior to about 1913 was accomplished with simple horsepower. The arrival around this time of 'the first engine' is remembered by at least one former stable lad, and by the end of the Great War, steam was the primary shunting power. The pilot, always an 0–6–0T, was kept extremely busy (a further crew had subsequently to be provided to keep it at work 24 hours a day) not only marshalling goods trains but also shunting the various factories. These included an artificial manure works, timber yards, ICI works, maltings etc., and on occasions the Stowmarket tank would also journey to Needham Market (the next station) shunting the maltings there at peak periods.

A 12,000 gallon water tank, at '£90-£100' and 'double its present capacity' was authorised for Stowmarket as early as 1883 and a supply of water raised by pumping engine and usually taken near to the signal box, was at first the only facility enjoyed by the pilot. On 5th February 1920 the Traffic Committee heard that 'there is at present no Engine Pit or Coal Stage at Stowmarket, and the enginemen have complained of the lack of pit accommodation and the heavy work involved in coaling engines'. Satisfying this requirement was estimated to cost £247. This pit, sited by the top of the 'up' sidings near to Prentice Bros. Artificial Manure Works, was subsequently home for the Ipswich tank engine, a 'J66' in 1931 and a 'J67' by 1951. H. D. Bowtell, writing in the *Railway Observer* of May 1937, comments on Stowmarket: '1 engine – yard pilot; stands in open on pit . . . when not in use. J66 7323.' In BR days at least, the men, though living locally, tended to be former Ipswich main line drivers, still with one of their number 'in charge'. Locos were changed periodically, not necessarily at weekends, the 'old one' returning on arrival of the 'new engine' from Ipswich. The practice continued until the end of steam, replaced by a diesel, which remained until the mid-1970s.

Parkeston shed in LNER days. The railway development here was nothing if not comprehensive, with station, quay, yards and shed. It was a lonely, dreary piece of coast and accommodation and new housing, some on a grandiose scale, was planned. They were drawn up during 1884 through to 1892 and beyond, with blocks of 28 to 32 cottages and even roundabouts in the new town.
Photomatic

PARKESTON

The Harwich branch from Manningtree was completed in 1854, experiencing a distinctly shaky early history until boat services began in earnest some ten years later. Facilities at Harwich itself were then rapidly developed — Messrs. Perry and Judson's tender of £6,480 was accepted in March 1864 for the 'new timber pier'. There was as yet no engine shed but locomotives appear to have stabled in a single road wooden 'Engine House' built close by the embankment to the west of Dovercourt station. This building, some half mile from Harwich, was in use at an early date — certainly before the end of 1864 and probably quite a while prior to that. On 1st April 1863 F. Bell's tender of £48 10s 0d was accepted for the 'Dovercourt Tank House'. There was no turntable although a 42 ft example, retained for decades even after Parkeston shed and its 'table were complete, was available more or less from the first, laid on a short spur just to the south of the Harwich terminus. In the 1870s at least some coaling, from wagons, took place alongside.

In this early period, provision for locomotives on the branch was obviously severely limited, giving rise to concern as early as June 1871: 'Harwich; water supply to Locomotive Engines: Locomotive Superintendent states we are badly off for water at Harwich both as to quality and quantity but a good supply could be obtained at Manningtree.' 'The Engineer' was then instructed to investigate matters, 'to furnish an Estimate for an Engine Shed and Turntable at Manningtree'. A curious notion, it disappears understandably promptly and operating problems continued to occupy the Way and Works Committee. On 19th July 1871 they heard that 'a large quantity' of water was available at Wrabness, the problem being that it was

five miles away and would cost £4,000-£4,500. Quite properly it was pointed out that it would be 'no good unless at Harwich'; Mr. Davis (Ipswich District Engineer) was instructed to 'investigate the Wrabness supply', but at the same time the Committee was quite clear, 'the cost cannot be incurred'. By 1876 the shed at Dovercourt may well have been suffering further problems. On 14th November the GE Law Clerk was instructed 'immediately' to take action against a local individual. He was evidently extracting 'mud and ooze' nearby with the unfortunate result that the 'Ticket Platform' was slipping and settling 'towards the sea'.

It was only a few years before the great Parkeston Quay project began to take shape. It involved the wholesale reclamation of 'Ramsey Ray Island' (the 'Isle of Ray') west of Dovercourt and a diversion of the branch in a great northward loop, for the quay was to stand by permanent deep water. A modern brick-built four-road shed, incorporating a substantial water tank at the rear (conforming to current GE thinking on such matters) was provided at the eastern end of the complex, the whole coming into use in March 1883. Dovercourt's 'Engine House' must necessarily have gone out of use (6th December 1881: estimate £7,220 for doubling line 'Parkeston Junction (Harwich End) to Dovercourt', including the rearrangement of the Dovercourt Station') though the Harwich turntable remained in place. The new shed was provided with a 50 ft turntable and a simple open coal stage on the west side. A 'Lighting Up Furnace', £35, and a pair of electric lights for engine pits, £90, were authorised in September 1893 and in 1912 a larger turntable was installed. It came into use at the beginning of December, having been approved on 21st March: 'The present turntable at Parkeston requires renewal. It is only 50 ft diameter and in view of the possibility of our

Parkeston on 28th March 1937. There were twenty-four engines at the shed that day, Nos. 1259, 2723, 2805, 2826, 2827, 2836, 2944, 2949, 2989, 2991, 2993, 7048, 7054, 7090, 7150, 7151, 7165, 7186, 7197, 7511, 7583, 7945, 8507 and 8508. Nos. 7196 and 7197 were at the docks, with 7185 in the station.

W. A. Camwell

new main line passenger engines working to that station it is desirable that in replacing it a turntable of 65 ft diameter should be put down. Required alterations = £1875, Turntable = £700.'

In the 1890s it seems that some provision was made for increased locomotive repair work,

Parkeston had a long association with the largest passenger engines available to the Great Eastern; the original 50 ft turntable was inadequate for the everyday use of these locos and a 65 ft under girder unit (probably locally built by Ransomes Rapier) was put in a short distance beyond the original 'table. 1st December 1912.   *K. Nunn/LCGB*

though with Ipswich so close, Parkeston never became a 'shop' as such. The following tenders for 'Locomotive Workshops' at Parkeston were examined on 20th May 1890:

F. Dupont, Colchester – £1275
John Saint & Sons, St. Ives, Hunts. – £1498
H. Everett & Sons, Colchester – £1545
A. Coe, Ipswich – £1580
Parkinson, Sleaford – £1628 13s 6d.

Messrs. Dupont, with the lowest bid, were naturally successful and their tender was accepted with alacrity. Whether or not there

was subsequently some delay is not clear, for there are references to a Messrs. Collins and Barber of Downham Market carrying out the work as late as 1896, for £1,460. On 3rd February 1891 the Locomotive Superintendent had submitted a list of machinery required for 'Parkeston Shops', a total of £1,314, of which the largest item was a 'Barrow Patent Screwing Machine', £210.

The location of this grandly equipped shop is not clear, either from plans or photographs – oft mentioned, it seems in fact not to have seen completion at all, or at least not in the form

No. 8040 in an ash-strewn yard.   *J. G. Dewing*

B12/1 No. 8507 on 16th July 1932. The first, No. 1500, had gone to Parkeston in 1912, following trials, with the first batch, 1501-1504, apparently following it later in the year. It is not clear if all were at work before the new turntable went in.   *Collection Michael Brooks*

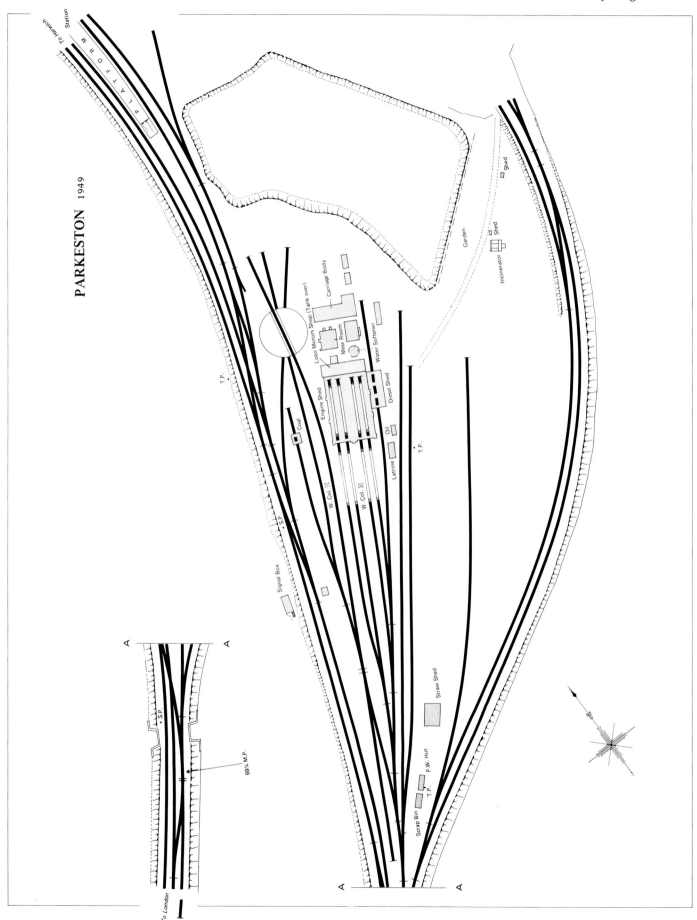

PARKESTON 1949

To Harwich Station
To Harwich

PLATFORM

T.P.

S.P.

Signal Box

Coal

W. Col.

W. Col.

Engine Shed

Loco Motors Shop (Tank over)

Carriage Body

Mess Room

Water Softener

Diesel Shed

Oil

Latrine

T.P.

Garden

Incinerator

Shed

Shed

Scrap Bin

P.W. Hut

T.P.

Straw Shed

A — A

A — A

S.P.

69¼ M.P.

To London

Parkeston on 17th April 1949. A coaler and water softener had been provided by this time; such things generally made life easier but there were always other problems — continued staff reductions for instance — to compensate. *T. J. Edgington*

envisaged in 1890. If such a shop was ever provided, it did not long survive the Grouping. A small brick lean-to was added in the 1940s to cater for the (then new) diesel shunters but no 'shop' then existed, though there are other references to its construction. A further intriguing reference comes on 15th October 1895 in a report to the Traffic Committee on a visit to Harwich. The 'Engineer' explains his plans for a warehouse 'now used by the Stores Department . . . and *the shed used for the loco*' [authors' italics]. The plan provided for 'the loco . . . being used by the Stores Department and for the Stores Warehouse to be added to and used as a Repairing Shop by the Loco Department'. Costs were estimated this time at £3,000, the work 'to be taken in hand with all speed'. The great part of the references to machinery and workshops in all probability relate to marine work.

Part of the Ipswich District, 'Parkeston and Harwich' (where traditionally several carriage cleaners, running dept. staff, were also engaged) occupied an important niche in the GER organisation, a prestigious post responsible for smartly timed expresses and a lucrative goods traffic. It had the use of some 30-40 locomotives, from the latest passenger and goods types through to various shunting tanks. 'B1' and 'B17' 4-6-0s, and 'K3' 2-6-0s, Britannia Pacifics and WD 2-8-0s worked regularly to Parkeston in LNER and BR days. Conventional engines rather than trams were preferred for the various dock turns, from 'Buckjumper' 0-6-0Ts up to 'J19' 0-6-0s at Harwich when the tide was low. Considerable force was then required for the lift out of the ferry, locos in excess of No. 5 route availability using several 'reach wagons' to avoid traversing the 'link-span'. Shunting on Parkeston Quay itself

Re-roofing in progress at Parkeston. The flat, low-lying nature of the reclaimed ground rendered it prey to flooding, most notably in 1953 when its locos were marooned in the shed or yard for some two weeks. The head of the yard where it ran close to the water had indeed long been a favourite spot for the resident Parkeston mute swans, and their successive offspring. In 1934 the *London & North Eastern Railway Magazine* even published a photograph of the family group, parents and cygnets against a background of the shed, supplied by 'Passed Cleaner L. Chisnall'. *W. Scutcher, courtesy R. Clow*

Parkeston station from the shed roof. The *Railway Magazine* of October 1957 commented on the importance of the place, noting that 'Claud Hamilton' 4—4—0s were only capable of successfully handling trains like the 'Hook Continental' if a select few were set aside for special mainten-ance. The new 4—6—0s were designed for this kind of job and on their introduction to Parkeston the magazine noted: "It may be recalled that this was in accordance with the time-honoured G.E.R. custom of shedding practically all its main line engines 'in the country': they normally worked up to London and back once or several times a day, and those kept at Stratford overnight were mostly visitors. The unusual arrangement had the advantage of minimising light engine workings between Liverpool Street and Stratford on already very congested tracks."

W. Scutcher, courtesy R. Clow

used in the main a system of hydraulic capstans dating from 1883. Dock turns thus did not figure greatly in the rosters, nevertheless diesel shunters arrived in the late 'forties, followed by BR 'dock' 0−6−0 diesel mechanical engines in the early 1950s; four, Nos. 11109, 11110, 11111 and 11113, were part of the allocation by 1954.

The shed building at Parkeston had deteriorated by BR days, much of the roof requiring recladding in corrugated material. The LNER had neglected the building itself but had carried out several steps designed to improve the working of engines. A lightweight girder frame coaling hoist was ordered from the Mitchell Conveyor and Transporter Company in September 1930 following a Locomotive Committee decision of 1st May to carry out unspecified 'improvements' to the value of £2,048. As well as the coaler, these included water softening apparatus, undervalued in 1930, for in January a total of £3,538 was approved for a new system, 'capacity 2600 gallons per hour'. The unit eventually ordered was capable

Train at Parkeston, with a background of the vaulted GE tank house. Similar trains, evidently, were a special feature of the Parkeston workings, a frequent service of five six-wheelers, the Parkeston-Dovercourt-Harwich workmen's shuttle service, hauled by J65 0−6−0Ts.

Dr. I. C. Allen

'The Dutch Boat' at Parkeston. Stratford 'Britannias' worked the 'Hook Continental', driven by Parkeston men — 'a most reliable bunch who came to duty early to clean the brass work on their own allotted locomotives'. J39 0−6−0s characterised freight working in the district and six were allocated in 1950; they were, however, 'considered a most unreliable beast'. They were responsible for much of the work in the early 1950s but were only thought suitable for the fast 'Goodmayes' for a few months after shopping. After that they were relegated to the cross-country Whitemoor jobs. B1 4−6−0s ran the Continental Reliefs, Day Continental, BAOR trains, stopping passengers, to both Liverpool Street and Peterborough.

A. Foster, courtesy R. Clow

The Parkeston allocation in 1950 was as follows: B1 4–6–0: 61003/4/5/6, 61135, 61232, 61264; J39 0–6–0: 64770, 64777, 64779, 64787, 64788, 64873; J15 0–6–0: 65446, 65458; J67/9 0–6–0T: 68500, 68561; J68 0–6–0T: 68643, 68649, 68653; N7 0–6–2T: 69612, 69614, 69621, 69635, 69677.

Collection V. Forster

0–6–0T No. 68500 at Parkeston around 1960, the coaling pilot.

Dr. I. C. Allen

Parkeston as diesel depot in 1961, showing the brick diesel shop originally built for work on the new shunters. The tank was for waste oil but of most note was the water softener weather vane, a three foot replica, in bronze, of the Gresley B17 *Sandringham*. Inside the shed is English Electric Type 4 No. D204; D200-D209 had ousted the 'Britannias' on boat and Norwich trains from 1958.   *R. Clow*

of providing 5000 gallons per hour and Kenni-cotts' tender of £1,070 was accepted on 28th March 1935. The tower etc. was erected later that year by the Yorkshire Hennebique Co. for about £1,000.

Passing into the clutches of Stratford after the Ipswich District was dismantled, Parkeston lost its steam allocation from January 1960. The turntable and the outer two of its four roads were removed, and diesels, both main line and shunters, continued to work from the shed. Parkeston seems not to have finally closed until the end of January 1967, after which it was demolished, to make way for new freightliner development.

Demolition, 1966/67. The dreary debris reveals all manner of detail.   *Collection R. Clow*

Bury shed. It was inevitably surrounded by maltings and, of course, relied heavily on agricultural traffic. Its status as a junction, however, left it relatively unscathed by the agricultural slump in the 1930s; only the general traffic decline of the late 1950s finished it as a railway centre. *National Railway Museum*

2−4−0 No. 7408 at Bury in 1936.

J. E. Kite

BURY ST. EDMUNDS

The Ipswich and Bury St. Edmunds Railway opened in 1846, extending to a more substantial station the following year. A plan of this terminus in 1847 (see Great Eastern Railway Society *Journal* No. 4 of September 1975) shows two tracks extended beyond the station to a small turntable, giving access to a single road engine shed. The Eastern Counties appeared in 1854, inaugurating through Cambridge-Ipswich working; subsequently lines from Long Melford (1865) and Thetford (1876) made Bury something of a country junction but the great part of its traffic remained east-west in nature. A considerable volume of goods grew up at Bury itself and an extensive yard with substantial goods shed was established. The original single road engine shed would necessarily have been removed in 1854, on arrival of the ECR line from Newmarket and presumably its replacement was erected more or less at once. It required repairs estimated at £250 in November 1871 and a variety of tenders were received, ranging from £150-£254. In accordance with normal practice, the former was accepted, from Messrs. Garlands. The shed was a relatively flimsy building, on the north side of the line west of the station. The turntable lay in the goods yard and by the early 1880s a siding led past the north side of the shed to give access to both a gravel pit and a variety of malthouses.

An 'extension of the Loco Sidings' was authorised on 3rd February 1891, at an esti-mated cost of £200, and in September 1893 further improvements were carried out; two extra engine pits and a splendid '6 ins. Swan neck Water column' to take advantage of a new supply 'from the tank by the Station'. Costs of this work were estimated at £220.

Executed in wood, the shed survived several decades of Great Eastern care, succumbing eventually to inclement weather conditions in 1901. In spring of that year, 'during a strong wind a portion of the roof of the present Engine shed at Bury was blown off leaving the shed in a more or less dangerous condition'. Remedial measures were in mind: 'Mr. Holden has for some time wanted a new shed there of larger capacity and thinks this a favourable opportunity to carry out the scheme. The existing shed is a wooden structure with a slate roof about 140 feet long and 35 feet wide . . . [it would] . . . not stand a new roof'. The estimate totalled £8,500, plus £612 for new 9 inch piping 'between the tank at the River' and (once again) the 'tank at the station'. On 18th November 1902 it was decided that 'Tenders will be dealt with by the Chairman'.

Almost nothing remained of the shed by now and throughout the following winter and that of 1903-4, engine preparation at Bury was a bleak business indeed. A 50 ft turntable had appeared, however, displacing the old goods yard unit; whether this predated Bury's disas-trous tempest or whether Holden had taken the opportunity to prise it from his reluctant directors is not clear. The three-road shed, its northlight pattern roof conforming to current GE practice, finally opened in 1904, a minimal delay in railway terms. Some indi-cations as to the costs are contained in the following reference, which must refer to some-thing other than simply water:

	Vote	Cost	Difference Under Over
Bury St. Edmunds – New Shed, Water Connections, etc. (N.B. one-third is chargeable to revenue)	£9112	£6444	£2668

Part of the Ipswich District, Bury was no simple outstation, having by 1914 over thirty men attached. W. Watson was the fitter-in-charge, responsible for the booking of engines and men, repairs to engines and correspondence. He directed the daily work of eight drivers, three acting drivers, six firemen, six acting fire-men, a boiler washer, a coalman, four cleaners, two examiners and a pair of pumpmen. By 1931 the remarkable total of seventeen engines is recorded working from Bury; by 1950 there were fourteen and in 1954 sixteen. Bury came under Cambridge when the LNER dismembered the Ipswich District and acquired Sudbury and Haverhill as sub-sheds. In 1937 an observer recorded fifteen engines on the complement, as follows: 'D2' 4−4−0 Nos. 4336 and 4366; 'D13' 4−4−0 No. 8025; 'E4' 2−4−0 Nos.

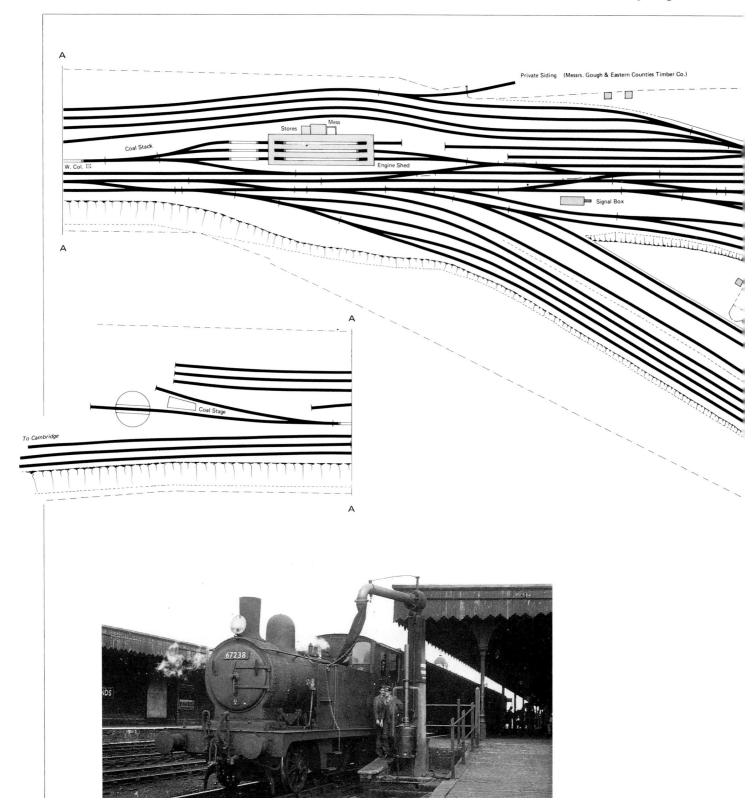

Cambridge 2—4—2T No. 67238 working out of Bury St. Edmunds. This was a Cambridge engine but such trains, unhurried rambles across Suffolk, typified the work at Bury shed.

Dr. I. C. Allen

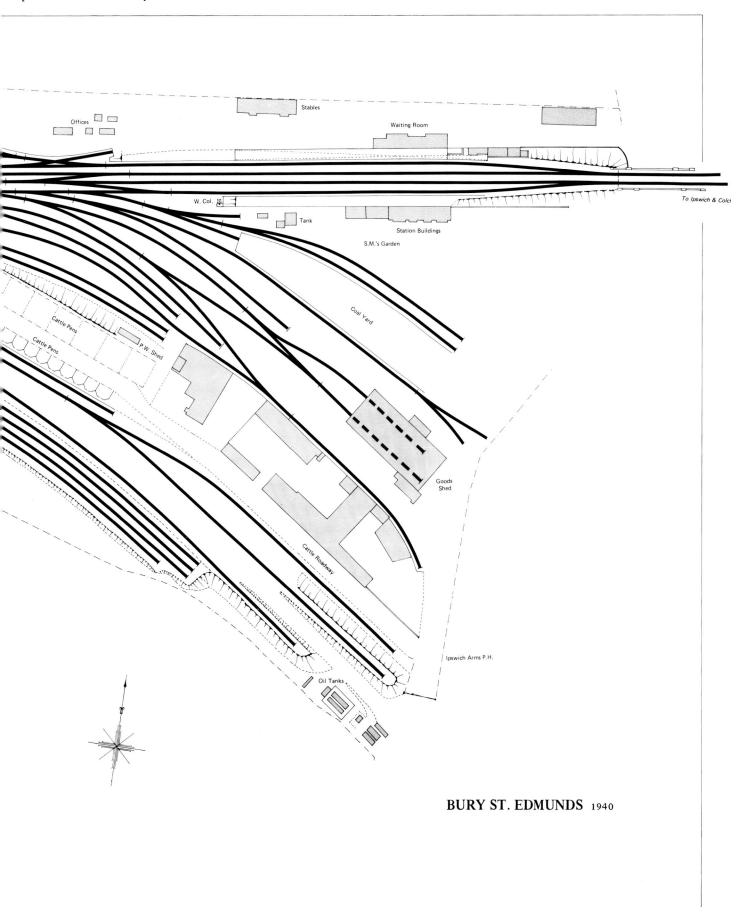

Offices

Stables

Waiting Room

W. Col.

Tank

Station Buildings

S.M.'s Garden

To Ipswich & Colchester

Coal Yard

Cattle Pens

Cattle Pens

P.W. Shed

Goods Shed

Cattle Roadway

Ipswich Arms P.H.

Oil Tanks

BURY ST. EDMUNDS 1940

Bury St. Edmunds on 4th May 1957, the twilight of cross-country running, relegated to ageing B12 4—6—0s.

B. K. B. Green

Bury on 8th October 1951. Traffic had peaked during the Second World War and Bury would never again achieve any national importance, in a transport sense. Vast amounts of matériel had passed through the place during the war years but its 50 ft 4 ins turntable had never been enlarged. Many 2–8–0 workings had terminated there – presumably there was light running to Newmarket or engines used the triangle on the Bury side of Newmarket tunnel. Bury St. Edmunds by 1951 had something of the 'after the storm' atmosphere about it.   *D. Clayton*

Timeless scenes could briefly return after the war; the clanking buffer sounds which seemed to travel (particularly at night) over such extraordinary distances. No. 68497 trundles by with a van in August of 1956.   *Dr. I. C. Allen*

Bury on 26th May 1957.

K. Fairey

J15 0–6–0 No. 65420 at Bury on 5th May 1957. The date upon which Bury St. Edmunds (and Sudbury) ceased to operate under direct Cambridge control is not known. Operationally the shed remained intimately connected with Cambridge and the 1866-67 notebooks of George Macallan (Cambridge DLS) leave no doubt that he was responsible for these 'outstations'.

B. K. B. Green

7409, 7421, 7458, 7467, 7479, 7503 and 7504; 'F3' 2–4–2T Nos. 8065 and 8073, 'J15' 0–6–0 No. 7924 and 'J69' 0–6–0T No. 7340. 'Claud' 4–4–0s remained at Bury through the 1950s, on passenger work, accompanied by 'J15s' on goods and various tanks, 2–4–2Ts, etc. for duties even more local in nature. 'E4' 2–4–0s were still there in 1947 and two as late as 1950, Nos. 62786 and 62795. There is indeed considerable detail available regarding the locomotives of Bury St. Edmunds, from early days to the end, and it is worth recording the following:1866-1867, sub-shedded from Cambridge (replaced by others when under repair): Sinclair V 2–4–2WT Nos. 153, 159; ex-EVR 2–2–2 Nos. 263, 266, 269, 270. In 1888 there were eight locos at Bury and in 1953 the complement comprised: 'D16' 4–4–0 Nos. 62513, 62541, 62543, 62566, 62607, 62615; 'E4' 2–4–0 No. 62783; 'J15' 0–6–0 No. 65420; 'F6' 2–4–2T Nos. 67222, 67236, 67238, 'J69' 0–6–0T No. 68497.

Some time prior to 1953 the shed acquired a new roof, a modification leaving the building very open and uncomfortable to work in. The northernmost road was used mainly for coal wagons, engines apparently being coaled direct. The water supply had continued to give trouble over the years – in June 1929 the Locomotive Committee had heard that 'the three interconnecting wells at the depot which yield about 26,000,000 gallons a year are inadequate for present requirements which are in excess of 45,000,000 gallons p.a.' The Committee accordingly authorised £520 for 'Messrs. Isler, the water experts' to take the necessary action.

Bury retained a marvellously Great Eastern atmosphere, despite the occasional '2MT' mogul, and apparently closed officially on 5th January 1959. It still stood, with decaying roof, as late as the following August, Type 2 diesels stabling on its pit roads.

Bury a year or two before recorded official closure. This apparently came (many of these East Anglian dates are vague) 'with introduction of new diesel services on January 5th 1959'. Other dates given include, in April 1959, 'since October last'. *J. H. Meredith*

The end of steam came with an awkward suddenness to the GE section, a deceptive hiatus before, with awful clarity, it was seen that diesels could not be an answer in themselves. An entire system of railway working, of which the Great Eastern was in so many respects typical, was irreversibly 'on the skids'. *W. T. Stubbs*

Colchester shed. It was cramped and ludicrously inadequate for the numbers of engines involved. It occupied an extremely elongated site, close to the main line and dangerous. The antiquity of much of the building convinced many staff that the offices and stores represented a pre-existing 'residence'. They were, in fact, the offices of the original single road depot retained for years after the shed itself had developed out of all recognition, rather after the fashion of Cambridge.

Collection W. A. Camwell

COLCHESTER

Colchester formed the western extremity of the Eastern Union Railway, operating in the early period as a terminus. It was a place of great importance for the EUR, its entire establishment, 'Station, Platforms, Engine and Carriage Sheds' valued in March 1849 at £1,000. Moreover, a third of the company's coke supplies were delivered at Colchester, the remainder at Ipswich (where facilities were valued at £1,500) an indication of the two sheds' relative importance. The Eastern Union had met the Eastern Counties head on at Colchester in 1846, making use of the latter's station opened in 1843 and, for a few years at least in this early period, the companies had separate engine sheds. The travails associated with the Eastern Union premises were numerous enough to ensure frequent attention in the minutes but the Eastern Counties shed is more obscure. A single reference of 14th August 1845 reveals a 'Smiths Forge with Bellows' ordered 'to be erected at the Colchester Engine House'. Presumably it stood to the west of the station, firmly on ECR property, but its

absence from plans of the late 1840s clouds the issue.

The EUR's shed had been opened more or less with the arrival of the company in Colchester in 1846 and it was as well that the buildings were indeed insured in 1849. On 28th January 1850 the Eastern Union's Traffic Committee heard 'that on the morning of the 25th instant, a fire broke out in the company's Engine House at Colchester by which 3 engines were injured and the Engine House completely destroyed'. An investigation into the cause of the disaster found it to have been simply 'accidental' in nature and notice was duly given by the Assistant Secretary to the Suffolk Fire Office, 'in which the building was insured'. The claim for £300 dragged on into the summer, being finally settled at only half that amount. To the irritation of the Committee, the 'Suffolk Fire Office' would not waiver from that figure, 'despite an intimation from the EUR that it would be prepared to settle at £200'. This sort of thing would ever plague the Eastern Union and after a period of indignities and bullying inflicted by its Colchester neighbour, it was rendered up to the aggressive ECR in 1854. (This of course took place on terms

dictated by the ECR – as early as January 1847 the Eastern Union chairman had been authorised to enter amalgamation negotiations). In May 1850 the ECR 'coaching Superintendent' had written that 'on or after the 1st proximo . . . it is intended to discontinue using the Pilot Engine at Colchester'. This effectively left the EUR without power for its Marks Tey service over ECR metals, 'this Company's Local Train, which arrives at Colchester at 4.30 p.m.' Following takeover, the working engines would necessarily have been concentrated in a single building but exactly how and when this was done is not clear. However, it was not long before a single road shed, east of the station amidst open fields, was in operation. Variously extended, repaired etc., it remained on this site until the end of steam.

Colchester at an early date became a depot of major importance, noteworthy for an inordinately high allocation coupled with a most modest layout. Overcrowding, even by GE standards, was extreme and the shed's entire history is a catalogue of grudging additions, always inadequate and invariably long overdue. To the eve of dieselisation Colchester was 'desperately small' with congestion such that at

Colchester shed occupied a narrow strip of ground on the north side of the line, beginning at North Street (by the Railway Tavern) and extending a considerable distance beyond the next bridge. This kind of site allowed the very least freedom of movement and made for a most awkward system of working. For years coaling was carried out from a low bank between the turntable and the shed which served as both coal 'stack' (see plan) and a coal stage. The Ordnance Survey reflected this confusion by labelling the area (rightly and wrongly, in different senses) 'Coal Yard'.

Collection P. W. Swinger

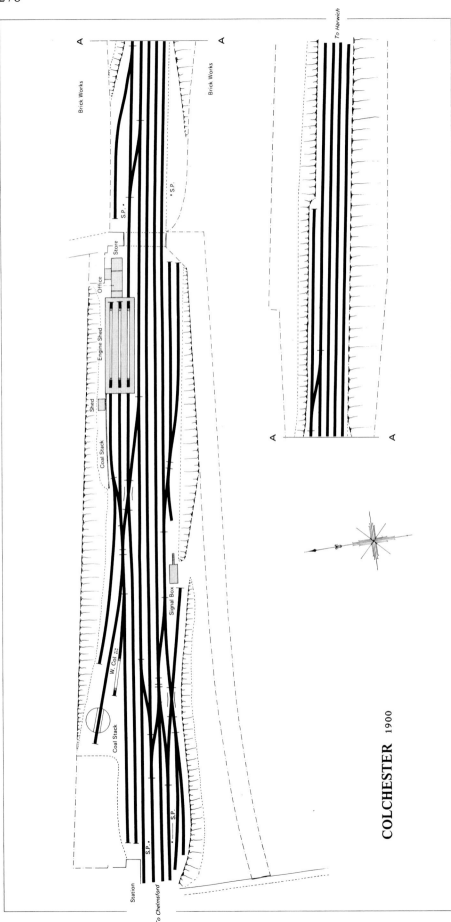

COLCHESTER 1900

weekends engines were of necessity often dumped in the goods yard.

It was the water supply, however, which at first occupied the GE authorities and in 1866 an agreement was reached with the Colchester Water Works Company for an improved supply, at £200 per annum for the ensuing five years. An increase in demand was foreseen, with further payments fixed at 8d per 1,000 gallons if the amount drawn exceeded 30,000 gallons per day, reducing to 6d per 1,000 gallons over 50,000 gallons a day. At the time the Traffic Committee noted that 'since 1864 we have paid £100 per year and £40 a year has been paid for water sent to Harwich in Tanks'.

The turntable was not well suited to the increasingly rigorous conditions at Colchester and early in 1869 proposals arose regarding its replacement. Johnson recommended a site but the whole idea was deferred on 17th February – 'it would not be adopted'. Only a week later, however, on 24th, officers paid a visit to Colchester and inspected the proposed site, the 'table to be 'in lieu of old one worn out'. It was decided to await yet another report from Johnson, 'to decide whether the new site should be chosen or the present one made use of with line from the Engine Shed in lieu of that out of the Main Line beyond the Turntable'. The detail of Johnson's report is now lost to us but it was eventually accepted, meeting with the approval of the Way and Works Committee on 3rd March 1869.

Further improvements were put in hand later in the year. In July 1869 the Locomotive Superintendent wrote . . . 'we have 6 Engines stationed at Colchester but there is only accommodation for 3 – thus 3 Engines have to remain outside the shed at night . . . I purpose a dead siding 150 feet long to be placed at the north end of the shed, to hold 2 Engines. This would provide for the safety of Engines in respect of preventing them being pushed foul of the main lines and the facing points would provide against the risk of runaway engines. It would also obviate another evil which exists viz:- one engine has at present to stand on the path of a level crossing of which obstruction is complained of and law proceedings threatened. Estimate £110'. This action was deferred 'until the next meeting for the Locomotive Superintendent to be present', when Johnson was obviously able to secure the money. The siding duly appeared and, in variously amended form, stabled a large part of Colchester's allocation through to the end of steam. One such amendment took place late in 1877, with £24 expended for 'Addition to Engine Shed Siding, Colchester. At present holds 8 engines to be increased so as to accommodate another engine which it is necessary to station there'. Locomotives continued to block the level crossing and further remedial action was ordered on 7th May 1878. £125 was considered sufficient 'to avoid the evil'.

Colchester and its various 'evils' figured in a General Manager's Report of June 1889. Concerned mainly with Stratford (see page 12), it recommended accommodation for a further nine engines at Colchester at an estimated cost of £3,500. This laudable aim took some time, of course, to translate into reality, and it was August 1890 before a tender was accepted, of one John Saint. Saint's price at £1,811, was

A favourite spot for the photographing of trains, there are innumerable records of up trains passing Colchester shed. B17 2839 passes on 4th August 1933; the shed had been built with a northlight pattern roof, removed between September 1921 and April 1922 (see *LNER Sheds in Camera* by John Hooper, OPC). The stepped 'blockhouse' outline appeared at some time afterwards. *Collection Michael Brooks*

East of the 'Coal Yard' and a further narrow extension of the constrained site, were two sidings for engines awaiting attention, repair, transfer or whatever. The through track continued over the footpath from Turner Road and any number of engines were stored awaiting attention. In the ancient 'Residence' were mess rooms, oil and general stores, and a fitting shop, poorly equipped. The sidings were in many cases standage for engines destined for Ipswich. *W. A. Camwell*

Mixed goods passing Colchester on 4th August 1933. The *Railway Observer* gives the following allocation for Colchester in 1936: 55, 63-5, 2720/ 2/4, 7077, 7139/61/4/9/86, 7214/9/68/91/3, 7327/34, 7517/23/40/58/67/8/74/86, 7645/6, 7888, 7925/41-3, 8025/40/6/60/7/74/6/81/2, 8153/81/9, 8200/14, 8513/8/33/8/67/76/8/80, 8799, 8813/22/8/46/67/71/97.   *Collection Michael Brooks*

Colchester in 1935.   *H. C. Casserley*

Class K2 Mogul at Colchester. A number found their way onto the GE Section and several ended up at Colchester.   *Collection P. W. Swinger*

well below the GE's own estimate and beat easily the highest tender, that of Rogers and Robson, Brentwood, of £2,667. Saint's efforts resulted in a new brick shed of three roads, with a slated northlight pattern roof, then currently finding favour. The new building was not the sort of endeavour to be lightly undertaken for £1,811 and the contractor made as much as possible of existing foundation work, floor, pit, etc. The original road became a through portion of the new shed, an increasingly cramped arrangement unaltered in its essentials through to the shed's demise.

Some tinkering with the water supply followed as the nineteenth century faded, a 'Reserve Reservoir' of 50,000 gallons in 1891 and an 'auxiliary supply' from Colchester Corporation Reservoir in 1901. The 1866 Agreement with the Colchester Water Works had evidently lapsed at some time for in May 1901 it was recorded that loco water had 'for many years' been obtained 'from Sheepen Farm'. It was, however, now 'quite inadequate' necessitating a return to institutional services.

Activity at Colchester was renewed during the Great War, the most notable outcome being a new 65 ft turntable. It was installed a few feet to the north of the old unit and on completion the approach siding was slewed across appropriately. The background is contained in a reference of 20th of June 1915: 'Owing to the present turntable having a diameter of only 43′ 9″ it is quite unsuitable for turning many Engines of the day now in use.' Extension rails had long been necessary and 'the extra strain this put upon the table added to the fact it has been many years in use it is frequently getting out of order. This seriously hampers our engine work at Colchester'. £2,635 was set aside for the new 65 ft 'table, the total to include unspecified 'improvements to coaling arrangements'.

In February 1917 further work was called for, in a rare insight into the dislocation wrought in wartime: 'extra accommodation required at Colchester . . . owing to the withdrawal of engines from stations near the coast at night, which has resulted in additional engines being stabled at Colchester shed'. £267 10s 0d was authorised for an extra siding and an engine pit 'at the country end' of the locomotive sidings. Throughout all the shed's long history, repairs etc. had increasingly to be carried out in the open, a dismal prospect only marginally improved in the post-war concern over working conditions. In April 1920 it was noted, a trifle late, that 'there is no suitable accommodation for mechanical staff at Colchester and their work has to be carried out in a lean-to shed and an old box wagon'. A grand new shop was to measure 18 ft by 38 ft and cost £300.

Colchester was extensively updated by the LNER and, although the work included a rebuilding of the shed itself, in a singularly ugly blockhouse style which the LNER had contrived somehow to make its very own, nothing was done to alleviate the main problem, lack of covered space. Within the constraints of the site and an ever-pressing impecuniosity, the LNER made a creditable stab at modernisation, carefully thought out adjustments to the sidings linked with mechanical coaler (insubstantial but a vast advance on the old 'coal yard'), new ash pit etc. Much of the scheme was described and approved (at a cost of £1,439) at the LNER Locomotive Committee meeting of 30th January 1930:

'Coaling of the 45 locos at Colchester is carried out by hand directly from wagons standing on an adjacent road, the quantity of coal consumed being about 350 tons per week.

'It is proposed that, in the interests of efficiency and economy, a modern coaling plant of tub elevator type, with ten 1-ton tubs should be provided, with the necessary track and coalmen's shelter. This would necessitate the removal of a siding on which coal wagons stand at the present time and to compensate for the space thus given up it would be necessary to extend one of the sidings at the east end of the yard for a length of 200 feet. The ashpit accommodation at the depot is inadequate and it is also proposed to extend the ashpit on the engine coaling road from 40 ft to 80 ft, the siding to be lengthened to accommodate an engine on the west side of the extended pit. Approved cost £1,439'.

The coaler was ordered from the Mitchell Conveyor and Transporter Co. costing (together with a similar unit for Parkeston) £1,610 and the programme duly went ahead, to culminate in a new water softener, a unit offering 3,300 gallons/hour and costing £3,294. The LNER period of reform apparently came to an end in 1936; on 1st October that year £1,157 'additional expenditure' was authorised for 'Revised arrangements with the Colchester Corporation in regard to water supply'.

Despite the embellishments detailed above, overcrowding and conditions in general at Colchester remained lamentable. The total of forty-five locos listed in the LNER report stood at an awesome sixty-one in December 1932:

The Colchester coaler, the lightweight tub elevator type installed at various sites throughout East Anglia.
British Railways

Colchester had a considerable goods working, handled in great part by 0–6–0s, mostly the smaller J15 engines. Only in the war and after were larger types available; the USA 2–8–0s were at Colchester before leaving for Europe and 'WDs' were around in the late '40s and early '50s. The USA engines were treated with some caution; the water gauge columns were said to give unreliable readings and this fault was blamed for injuries to an Ipswich crew caused by a blowback. There was also sometimes confusion over the nut types, which were similar enough to be mistaken for the home-grown variety. Several delays thus ensued.

H. N. James

Colchester on 20th May 1951. The previous year the allocation was listed as: B12 4–6–0: 61512, 61523, 61555, 61556, 61557, 61558; B2/17 4–6–0: 61603 *Framlingham*, 61607 *Blickling*, 61614 *Castle Hedingham*, 61615 *Culford Hall*, 61616 *Fallodon*, 61632 *Belvoir Castle*, 61639 *Norwich City*, 61644 *Earlham Hall*; E4 2–4–0: 62791; J15 0–6–0: 65424, 65432, 65440, 65441, 65443, 65445, 65448, 65456, 65465, 65468, 65473; J17 0–6–0: 65522, 65531, 65539, 65564; F4/5 2–4–2T: 67188, 67189, 67190, 67191, 67194, 67195, 57196, 67204, 67215, 67217; F6 2–4–2T: 67221, 67236, 67237, 67238; J67/9 0–6–0T: 68522, 68578, 68608, 68616, 68636, 68638; WD 2–8–0: 90029, 90085, 90431, 90443, 90471, 90477, 90508, 90522, 90732 *Vulcan*.

W. Potter

'B12' 4–6–0: 8513, 8518, 8533, 8537, 8538,
    8567, 8578
'D13' 4–4–0: 7737, 7745, 7756
'D15' 4–4–0: 8828, 8829, 8846, 8867, 8870,
    8871, 8897
'D16' 4–4–0: 8781, 8813
'E4' 2–4–0: 7473
'F3' 2–4–2T: 8046, 8067, 8074, 8076, 8081
'F4' 2–4–2T: 7077, 7574
'G4' 0–4–4T: 8105, 8109
'J15' 0–6–0: 7517, 7540, 7558, 7567, 7568,
    7600, 7642, 7645, 7646, 7690, 7924, 7925,
    7926, 7927, 7942, 7943
'J16' 0–6–0: 8181
'J17' 0–6–0: 8153, 8200, 8231
'J20' 0–6–0: 8283
'J65' 0–6–0T: 7248, 7254
'J66' 0–6–0T: 7293
'J67' 0–6–0T: 7327, 7332, 7334
'J68' 0–6–0T: 7048
'J69' 0–6–0T: 7268
'K2' 2–6–0: 4631
'Y3' 0–4–0T: 63, 64

2–4–0 No. 62789 on the Colchester turntable. Great Eastern types remained in some numbers at Colchester until dieselisation and electrification. Three ex-LTSR 4–4–2 Ts were there in 1956, 41936, 41939 and 41975; Stratford could find nothing useful to do with them and the situation is likely to have been the same at Colchester.   *H. N. James*

This was perhaps a less than welcome aspect of the improvement work though a considerable proportion of the stock was for much of the time out of the way at various sub-sheds. These had always been numerous and occupied in GE days almost as many staff, about seventy, as the main shed itself. Colchester was part of the Ipswich district in 1914 responsible for 'power as required for certain branches, viz:' Kelvedon, Witham, Maldon, Braintree, Brightlingsea, Clacton, Walton on Naze, Sudbury and pumping stations, Marks Tey, Thorpe le Soken, and Long Melford.

By 1931 the pumping stations and Witham no longer qualified as 'outstations' but the former independent sheds at Haverhill and Halstead had been taken aboard. Further alterations left the 'sub sheds' at five by July 1939; Braintree, Clacton, Kelvedon, Maldon and Walton. All survived well into the BR period.

An exhausting war had left the depot dilapidated and rundown with full scale renewal delayed as electrification to Clacton and Walton made its inching progress. By the end of summer 1960 dieselisation and electrification was far advanced (an official closure date of 2nd November 1959 exists) and diesel fuelling from tank wagons was underway at the shed; steam had almost entirely disappeared. One of the first modern diesel depots was subsequently opened at Colchester to service railcar sets and the Type 2 and 3 locos used in the district.

61655 *Middlesbrough* with a down Clacton train on 15th June 1957. The footpath ran from Turner Road and was a means of access to the shed and its 'Residence'. The through road (they were numbered 1-3 northwards) marks the site of the single road shed, whilst a later fitting shop is just out of sight to the right. This had a bench/vice and a 'foot lathe', 'more suited to wood turning and not often used', and was staffed by three fitters and a boilersmith and four assistants under a chargehand fitter. One of the fitters and a mate (on early turn) were generally found at either Braintree or Maldon, the driver having sent in the repairs list so that suitable tools could be taken.   *G. R. Mortimer*

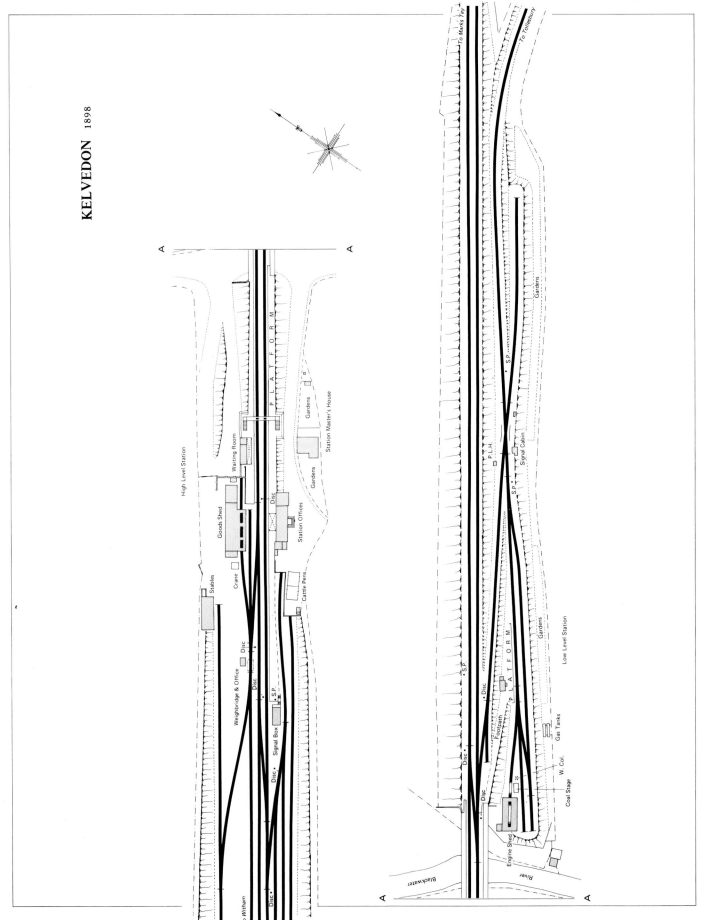

KELVEDON 1898

To Marks Tey

To Tollesbury

High Level Station

Stables

Crane

Goods Shed

Weighbridge & Office

Waiting Room

Disc

Disc

Disc

Disc

S.P.

Signal Box

Station Offices

Cattle Pens

Gardens

Gardens

Gardens

Station Master's House

To Witham

Disc

Gardens

S.P.

Disc

P.L.H.

Signal Cabin

S.P.

Low Level Station

S.P.

Disc

P L A T F O R M

Footpath

Gardens

Gas Tanks

W. Col.

Coal Stage

Disc

Engine Shed

River

Blackwater

KELVEDON

The light railway from Kelvedon to Tollesbury opened in October of 1904 with an extension to Tollesbury Pier in 1907. A shed was required for the single engine which was to work the line and the basic requirements were met, at minimum cost, by a tiny single road building in concrete with corrugated sheeting. A water tank standing on cast iron columns was provided alongside the shed; in November 1902 the 'proposed water supply for engines' at Kelvedon had been estimated to cost about £750 and in July 1903 the tender of the Ashton Green Iron Company £220 had been accepted for a 10,000 gallon tank 'at Kelvedon'. An outstation of Colchester, the shed housed no more than a single 0–6–0T for the great part of its existence. This confirmed a GE verdict of October 1901 – several estimates regarding the new line had been discussed including one of £12,216 dating from June 1898 and one of August 1901, totalling only £2,510. Kelvedon it was recorded, was . . . 'not a progressive place'.

Four men, a driver, acting driver, and two acting firemen, were based at Kelvedon for many years with very little in the way of com-

Kelvedon, 'not a progressive place'.   *Collection Michael Brooks*

The branch tank, No. 391, at its self-contained roost, 31st March 1910.   *Ken Nunn/LCGB*

The Kelvedon & Tollesbury terminus lay close by the main line but the short incline took one down into largely another world. Only the Great Eastern could run a line on jam.

Collection Michael Brooks

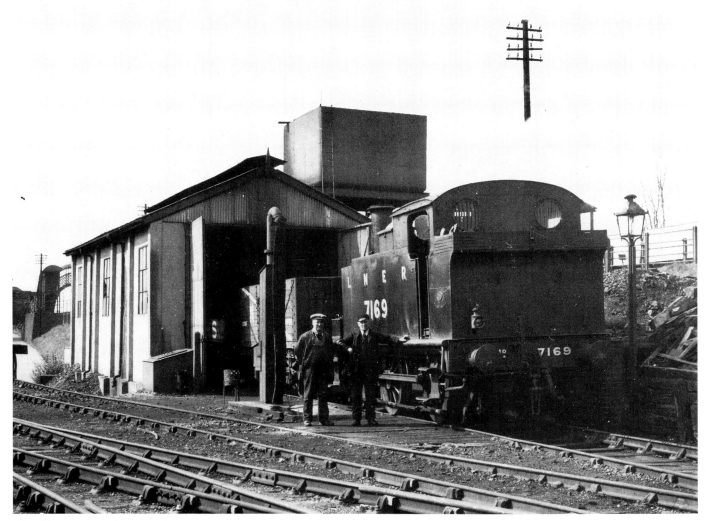

J67 No. 7169 at Kelvedon on 27th March 1937. The engine came back to the main depot at intervals but as at other small sheds in the district, a fitter would come out and attend minor adjustments or whatever. Even in the 'thirties the place was considered 'quaint'.   *W. A. Camwell*

fort: '3rd June 1919. There is no accommodation at Kelvedon for enginemen and cleaners for their meals or for the branch engine driver to book up his runnings. Is desirable to have a building for these men. Estimate £102. Approved.' The Kelvedon tank continued to trundle to and fro, mixing the handful of stalwart customers with peas, jam, and other sundry agricultural items.

The passenger service ceased in May 1951 and it was no longer necessary to outstation an engine – the shed closed and was afterwards demolished.

Kelvedon low level in 1950. The passenger service ceased the following year and the shed was quietly done away with.   *K. Nunn/LCGB*

WITHAM

There does not appear to have been more than a turntable, 42 ft with lengthening irons, a siding and perhaps a coal stage at Witham, though in the summer of 1914 no less than nine staff were based at this 'branch'. The 'loco dept' men, two drivers, two firemen and a cleaner, were supervised from Colchester but the remaining four, wagon examiners and greasers, were responsible to wagon foreman Clark at Ipswich.

Any thought of Witham as a 'shed' disappeared quickly under LNER rule though engine facilities at the junction seem to have undergone sustained improvement – no less than £1,001 was approved on 25th January 1934 'for electrification of the pump at Witham to enable the removal of three pump attendants.

At present water is pumped into the 40,000 gallon tank from a Spring on the Braintree branch and from a reservoir at Cressing by means of two steam pumps.'

At the end of March 1946 the Locomotive Committee recommended a further £1,909 for an improved locomotive water supply from the River Brain whilst earlier in the year, in January, it had approved a new 70 ft articulated turntable '. . . on the same site, with inspection pit and spur road . . . at £6,268'. This work was part of the LNER post-war reconstruction programme, but whether carried out or no, the

Witham turntable remained in use until September 1962. There had long, it appears, been no regularly allocated loco, engines being borrowed from the Colchester, Maldon or Braintree complements.

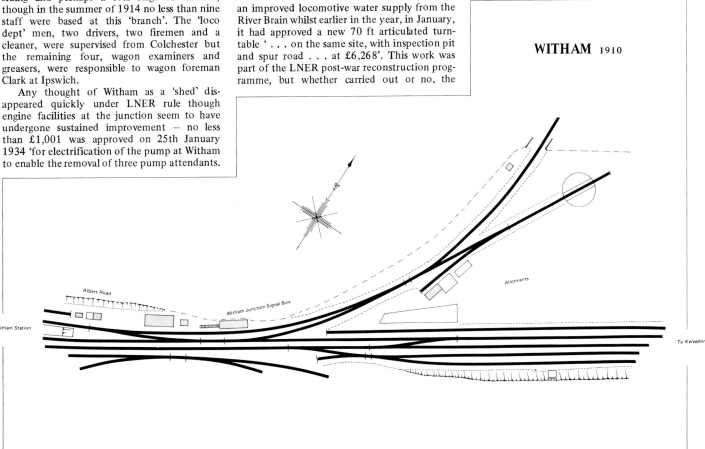

WITHAM 1910

Albert Road

Witham Junction Signal Box

Witham Station

Allotments

To Kelvedon

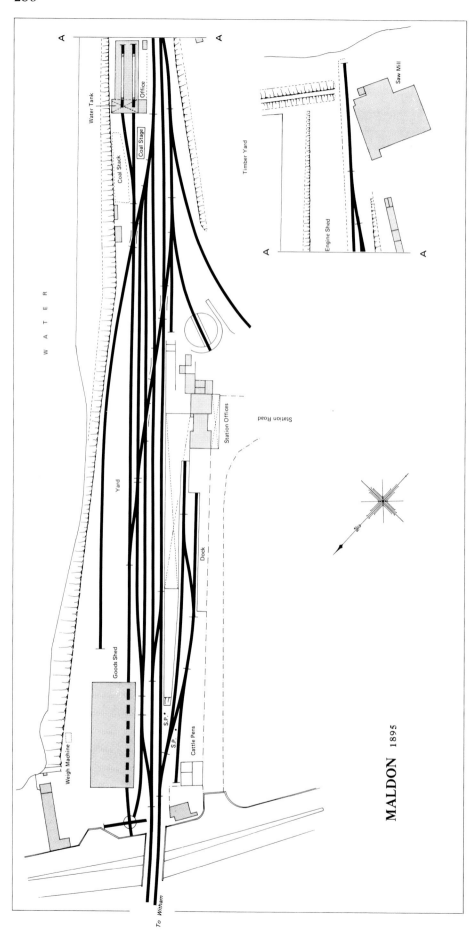

MALDON 1895

MALDON

Grandly and deservedly labelled 'Engine House', Maldon opened with this early Eastern Counties branch in 1848. The two road building was generously proportioned, with arched entrances and a substantial water tank, thoroughly in keeping with the elegantly laid out terminus.

Locomotives on the branch have been exhaustively listed in a Great Eastern Railway Society *Journal* article of July 1977, by P. Goldsmith. 2–2–2s, 2–4–0s, etc., appear to have been used in the early years, with 0–4–4Ts and 2–4–2Ts later coming to prominence on passenger work. The latter in particular held sway over many decades. Much heralded saviours of branch line services, German Waggon und Maschinenbau railbuses arrived in 1958 together with conventional railcars and Type 1 Bo-Bos on goods.

Maldon had for many years been without a turntable, though at first undersized goods tables were available about the yard. A proper engine turntable was considered desirable on completion of the new line in from Woodham Ferrers in 1889 and a 50 ft Ransomes Rapier unit was installed on the west side of the line in that year.

Two locos were at Maldon in the 1880s but up to three were in use throughout LNER days, a pair of 'F4' 2–4–2Ts accompanied intermittently by an 'F7' or an 0–6–0T. All were outstationed from Colchester where main repairs etc. were carried out, but in GE days at least the Maldon tanks were washed out locally. A boiler washer to this end accompanied the eight Maldon footplatemen (two drivers, two acting drivers and four acting firemen) and he doubtless carried out most other shed tasks in between coaling, loading ash, a spot of cleaning, etc.

The line closed to passengers in September 1964 and although steam had continued to show itself on goods work after the introduction of railbuses in 1958, it was not long before diesels had taken over completely. Maldon was reportedly made sub-shed to Parkeston 'from 2nd November 1959' and it is unlikely to have survived through much of the following year.

Locomotives in the last years included 'J15' 0–6–0 No. 65445 in May 1958, 'F5' 2–4–2T No. 67195 in February, and two 'J68' 0–6–0Ts, apparently sub-shedded at Maldon and working freights. No. 68666 and No. 68648 respectively in September 1956 and March 1957 were observed to run 'light to Witham, collect a goods, return to Maldon, shunt the yard, take the outgoing traffic to Witham and finally run light engine back to Maldon'. Other 'F5s' working from Maldon in 1956-1958 included Nos. 67212 and 67214.

Maldon was another agricultural line, and into the 1950s J68 tanks would inch their way out with entire train loads of canned fruit. The branch tanks (2−4−2Ts for years) pottered up and down to Witham or wherever but there was also a through service from Liverpool Street; it ran in the 'thirties, Saturdays only, a J15 0−6−0 with a suburban set. They were not Maldon engines (7643 and 7649 were observed, among many others) and in 1950 E4 2−4−0 No. 62791 was sent to Stratford to work the 12.53 p.m. Liverpool Street-Maldon Saturdays-only train. It ran non-stop to Shenfield but fared little better than the 0−6−0. No larger locos could be used on the branch. *Collection Michael Brooks*

The shed had only really been busy during the Second World War when troop and material movements forced crews to sleep overnight, on a table in an attached room. The Colchester fitter travelled out once a week to attend the engines, a couple of F4s, in 1950 Nos. 67191 and 67195. Early locos known to have worked from Maldon in the period 1863-1866 were: Nos. 87 and 135, both 2−4−0s, the latter ex-Norfolk Railway, 142, a Sinclair 'V' class 2−4−WT and No. 600, a 2−2−2. The following were recorded by Canon C. S. Bayes in the 1930s: 1932 − G4 8109; 1933 − G4 8105; 1934 − J65 7151; 1935 − F4 7077; 1936 − F4 7574; 1937 − F4 7586; 1938 − F4 7574/86; 1939 − F4 7574/78; 1940 − F6 7007; 1942 − F5 7144. *Collection Michael Brooks*

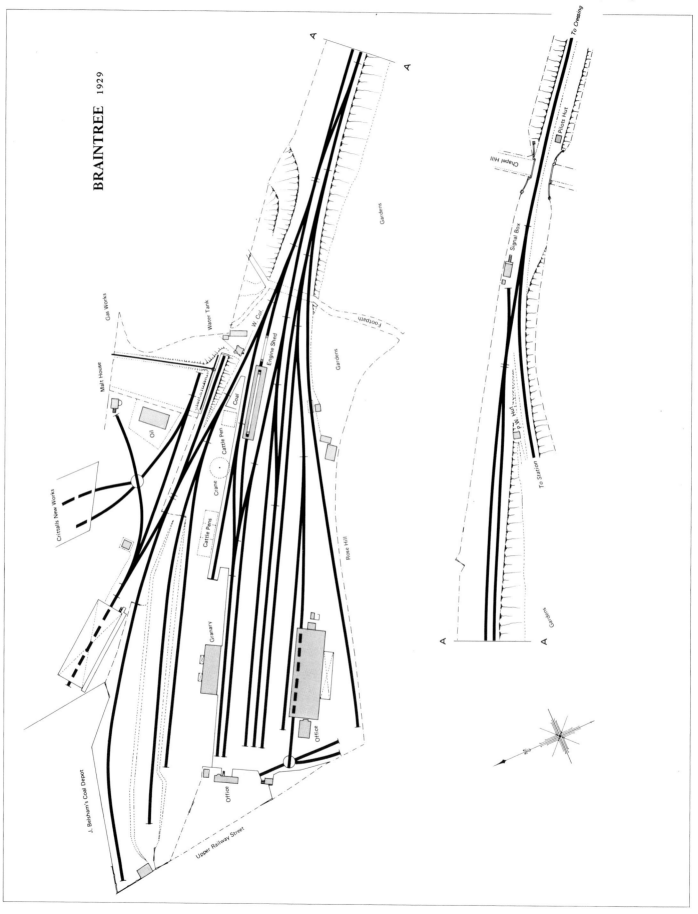

BRAINTREE 1929

Gas Works

Malt House

Water Tank

W. Col.

Crittalls New Works

Oil

Cattle Pen

Coal

Engine Shed

Crane

Cattle Pens

Gardens

Footpath

Gardens

Rose Hill

J. Belsham's Coal Depot

Granary

Office

Office

Office

Upper Railway Street

A
A

A
A

Gardens

To Station

S.W. Hut

Signal Box

Chapel Hill

Pilots Hut

To Station

To Cressing

Gardens

BRAINTREE

The shed at Braintree stood close by the original terminus of the line from Maldon and Witham, opened in 1848. The shed might well have been built at this early date but is not mentioned even in GE records of 1869, when the extension on to Dunmow and Bishops Stortford occupied the company. The old station was abandoned and a second one erected on the new through line, the old terminus serving usefully as a goods yard etc. A turntable, apparently for the first time, was now required at Braintree: '7th January 1869. Turntables are necessary at Bishops Stortford and Braintree if the trains do not run through to Witham.' '23rd February 1869 – Certificate issued for the line by the Board of Trade on the undertaking that until an Engine Turntable is provided at Braintree the Traffic shall be worked to and from Witham Station.' Three locos were allocated in 1888, with accommodation for only two.

A misfortune befell the little shed in 1909. The yard, busily occupied by day with agricultural goods, domestic coal etc., was enduring the latest and fiercest of that winter's gales when the timbers of the ageing wooden building at last gave way. The mournful story is told in a series of minutes dating from 1909 and 1910.

Braintree on 6th June 1938, with Nos. 8082, 7164 and, taking coal, No. 8067. The latter task was more usually carried out by the night shift cleaner.   *W. A. Camwell*

No. 67225 taking water at Braintree.   *Dr. I. C. Allen*

The rest of the winter following the mishap and a great part of the succeeding one were endured before the accommodation was finally replaced. It may even have taken longer than that for the final references are dated December 1911.

'16th December 1909. Braintree Engine Shed . . . blown down by a heavy gale of wind at 4.00 a.m. on the 3rd instant and completely demolished. The shed (85' x 15') was constructed of wood, standing on a brick footing and had a slate roof. There were two engines in the shed at the time and the acting firemen on duty were in the act of working them out when the shed collapsed and a portion fell on to No. 1301 but only slight damage was caused to the paint work and cab top. No one was injured.
'6th October 1910 . . . Locomotive Superintendent . . . has been into the question [of the shed's reconstruction] with the Engineer and recommends that a new shed be provided at an estimated cost of £445 . . . will be 100 feet in length or 15 feet longer than the old one in order to accommodate two engines and will be erected on the site of the original shed so that the existing pits will be available. The old shed is estimated to have cost £255 exclusive of permanent way and engine pits . . . Approved.
'15th December 1910 – Tender of Clark and Sons £398 10s 0d. accepted for new Braintree shed.
'21st December 1911 – Works Complete – Braintree new Engine Shed Cost £190.' [The reasons for the disparity in cost is unknown.]

What might be termed 'basic provision', the shed was solidly founded with a new low roof and was able to survive the climatic vicissitudes of the following decades. One of Colchester's many 'Branches', Braintree enjoyed a staff of nine in 1914, a pair of drivers, two acting drivers, four acting firemen and a boiler washer. Tank and tender classes were at the shed in GE days, the latter, 2–4–0s, involved at one time on through trains to Liverpool Street. During the LNER period, however, into the 1950s, 2–4–2Ts were the usual inhabitants. Colchester normally outstationed a handful together with some kind of tank for goods shunting or indeed almost anything. In 1937 the following were working from Braintree: 'F3' 2–4–2T Nos. 8046 and 8070, 'F4' 2–4–2T No. 7475 and 'Y1' 0–4–0T No. 64. In the 1950s a single Colchester 2–4–2T was customary, together with an 0–6–0T 'J68' etc. In October 1954 a pair of 'F5' 2–4–2Ts and a 'J69' 0–6–0T reportedly formed the usual complement. Early in the 1950s the shed chargeman at Maldon was made responsible for both sheds and once again precise closure details are difficult to obtain. Many of these smaller sheds remained 'open' after the introduction of diesels – a German railbus was tried without success in the late fifties, and shortly before final closure (apparently around the end of 1959), railcars from Cambridge took over from steam.

Braintree on 5th May 1957, with No. 68663. About a century before, on 4th December 1863, an outside cylinder 2–4–0 of 1847, No. 82, was at the shed and in the period 1889-1891 the two pioneer Johnson 4–4–0s Nos. 305 and 306 were there, for through workings to Liverpool Street. They were replaced by 'T26' locos Nos. 425 and 426. Engines for local trips to Witham and so on were Johnson 'No. 1' class 2–4–0s, replaced by Holden E22 (J65) 0–6–0Ts Nos. 156 and 157 in 1889.

Collection John Hooper

BRIGHTLINGSEA

Brightlingsea, even in its rebuilt form, was an unexciting place, 'very bleak and cold', with traffic to match — 'oysters, sprats, general OUT, coal & shops goods IN'. 28th March 1937.
W. A. Camwell

The bleak and little known line from Wivenhoe to Brightlingsea opened on 18th April 1866. Despite the cajoling of the Great Eastern, who were to work the line, the Brightlingsea company declined to provide an engine shed, the station in addition remaining a dismal and inadequate structure. The GE purchased the line in 1893 but forgot the earlier requirements and at first made no engine shed provision. The old station burnt down at the end of 1901 and a new terminus on a site a few yards to the south was subsequently erected. A new one-road shed also appeared, in contemporary GE turn-of-the-century style, on a spur close by the old station.

This little brick shed bore somewhat unhappily a northlight pattern roof and would obviously have emerged entirely differently if GE promptings had been successful nearly forty years before:

'9th May 1866. Brightlingsea Railway Co. Accommodation required by the Locomotive Superintendent (of the Great Eastern) at Brightlingsea will cost for a Timber Shed £325 and if built in Brick £455 and the water supply is being laid on by the Contractors. Resolved, that the [Brightlingsea] Company be informed of the Estimate with a recommendation that the Shed be made in brick and that they be required to bear the expense'.

Later in June the GE was assured that the Brightlingsea directors 'were resolved that the Engine Shed be erected'. Despite such a declaration, nothing (apart from a tank and platform) had appeared by March 1867. The Locomotive Superintendent on 28th of that month complained of Brightlingsea tardiness: 'It is of

By 1949 the shed was more or less derelict, the northlight pattern roof, built strictly in accordance with Great Eastern turn of the century practice, having deteriorated severely.
T. J. Edgington

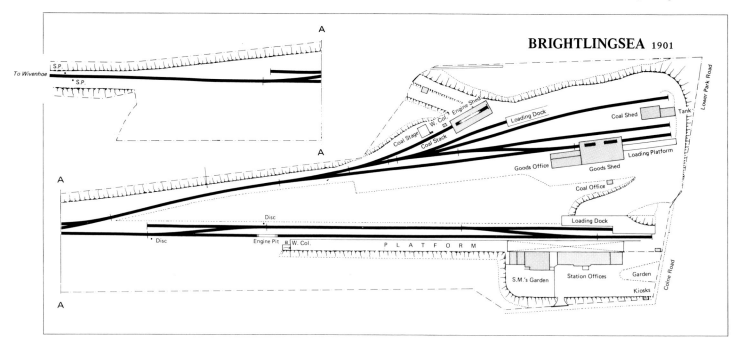

BRIGHTLINGSEA 1901

the utmost importance to have an Engine Shed at Brightlingsea and also provision made for washing out. The Brightlingsea line has been open about 12 months and nothing has been done to provide accommodation for want of which the Engine stationed there does not get properly attended to and the place is very bleak and cold.' The Secretary then reported that tenders had been 'determined' on 31st July *1866* but the Brightlingsea company objected to the cost (£483) and unfortunately 'had never given an undertaking to bear the cost which they are bound to do under the Agreement with this Company.' It was then resolved 'to call the attention of the Wivenhoe and Brightlingsea Co. to the stipulation in the Agreement and inform them that it is imperative that the Shed be erected without any further delay.'

After this there is an apparent readiness by the Brightlingsea people to accommodate the Great Eastern: Mr. Bradley, secretary of the W & B, replied that his board would examine the proposals 'very shortly' and on 24th April the company intimated their agreement 'as soon as the Estimates are settled'. 'The Engine Shed' seems finally to have been abandoned later in the year, however, with a ploy involving a conversion to *horse* haulage. '5th June 1867. With reference to Brightlingsea Engine Shed the matter has been referred to the [GE] Board on Thursday next to decide whether the line shall be worked by Engine power or horse power.' The Great Eastern seem to have given up after this and the branch engine presumably remained 'improperly attended to'. In November of 1867 there were lengthy discussions regarding a GE takeover of the branch, concluding that the line was really in not quite good enough condition, particularly the ballast. Accommodation at Brightlingsea itself was 'very poor'.

The shed had only two crews in late Great Eastern days and, despite its relatively late provision, was never more than a marginal establishment. As a sub-shed of Colchester, it settled down to a long period of 2–4–2T passenger haulage, 'F3s', 'F4s', etc. with 0–6–0s and 0–6–0Ts on goods work. A single tank

('F3 No. 8041 in early 1937') comprised the normal allocation through much of the LNER period. Economically the branch remained a dismal prospect; the LNER even considered its conversion to 'a motor road'. It was not considered worthwhile; despite much of the yachting having disappeared and the repairing business at a 'low ebb', passenger traffic was, nevertheless, described as 'of considerable volume'. In the year ending June 1932 receipts totalled £5,424 with freight described as 'oysters, sprats, general OUT coal and shops goods IN'. The booked annual train mileage Wivenhoe-Brightlingsea was 36,760 with the passenger trains 'except in 2 cases on weekdays' running through to St. Botolphs and/or Colchester.

Economies in prospect again came under consideration on 25th May 1939. Examined

along with a much larger and more venerable GE establishment, Peterboro' it was recorded: 'Brightlingsea depot is much smaller, only stabling one engine which works passenger trains between Brightlingsea and Colchester. By changing the type of certain engines allocated to Colchester depot, and by incurring some additional light mileage, it will be possible for Colchester engines to work the traffic and for a net annual saving of £638 to be effected'. 'No decision' was recorded following this report but it seems really to have spelt the end of the shed. It is absent from the LNER lists of July 1939 though the building, its smoke vents collapsing through ruinous roofing, still stood as late as 1960. The interior was wired off and the approach road host to a permanent way trolley.

The shed as P.W. depot, 2nd September 1960.   *W. T. Stubbs*

CLACTON

The railway into Clacton from Thorpe-le-Soken did not open until 1882. The original shed, an insubstantial single road affair measuring about 50 ft by 20 ft, would appear to date from the same year; it stood on the west side of the station, single-ended with a turntable alongside and a simple open coal stage. This at least was the position by 1890 when one engine only was allocated; by 1921 the road had been extended through the shed, a couple of tanks provided by the entrance and an additional siding laid in. This might well have been related to the events of early 1914: 'engines are occasionally coaled from wagons which necessitate them standing foul of the road leading from No. 4 platform to the shunting spur road. Recently whilst work of this description was in hand a collision occurred between an engine which was being loaded and another engine running toward the shunting spur . . . to obviate a recurrence . . . a new siding . . . recommended. £234 0 0.'

Some time in this period there is also a possibility that the shed itself was extended to

the rear, traces of walls appearing on plans of 1921. What did remain of the shed was, however, subsequently destroyed, blowing down, it appears, in a storm prior to 1927. A new shed was subsequently provided, part of a general station reordering carried out in 1928-1929. It remedied in some small measure long years of neglect and was erected to the north, facing the station and again on the west side of the line. Additional sidings etc. for the station occupied the old shed site and the turntable was also renewed. The whole was the outcome of a 1927 Committee of Inspection, prompted in its turn by lengthy consideration of the lamentable situation at Clacton. Efforts towards the relief of the primitive conditions had begun at least the previous year:

'Clacton 29th April 1926. The Divisional Manager reported that the existing turntable at Clacton which is only 45' 6" in diameter, is in such a condition that it is beyond effectual repair, and it is necessary that its replacement should be taken without delay. Plan No. 13364 submitted shows a scheme for providing a 70 ft turntable and siding on a new site. This would fit in with a com-

prehensive scheme which has been for some time under consideration for improving the accommodation at Clacton. The estimated cost of the work is £2,964. Resolved: that a 60 ft turntable be provided instead of a 70 ft and that the cost be reduced accordingly.'

The LNER chose to erect the new shed in wood planking on a timber frame over a dwarf brick wall. Doors were considered unnecessary, the coal stage was grimly traditional and the new Clacton depot could hardly have been considered advanced. The local water was probably amongst the worst in the south of England in terms of quality and, bizarrely, had not been available before 1914: '16th July 1914. Is no water at Clacton and when, as frequently happens, engines require water, they have to run to Thorpe-le-Soken or their trains stop there.' The reference goes on to note that despite a local council stipulation that the supply may be cut off in the summer in preference to local householders, a mushroom tank of 2,000 gallons capacity should be installed, at a cost of £275. The quality remained abysmal, alleviated only by a new water softener approved on 4th January 1934. Costing £2,556,

The original Clacton shed, probably around the time of the 1914 accident (above). The allocation grew from the original single engine, as commuter traffic increased, whilst the holiday peaks became greater every year. Rebuilding became necessary: "The remarkable growth of Clacton-on-Sea is very largely due to the excellent train service with which the Railway Company has endeavoured to popularise that resort. To meet the needs of the rapidly growing population of Clacton, to facilitate the working of the heavy summer service of excursion trains, and to provide greater comfort, not only for the excursionists, but also for the ever increasing number of season-ticket holders who travel to London daily, it had become necessary to construct an up-to-date station and to re-equip and re-model the yards." *National Railway Museum*

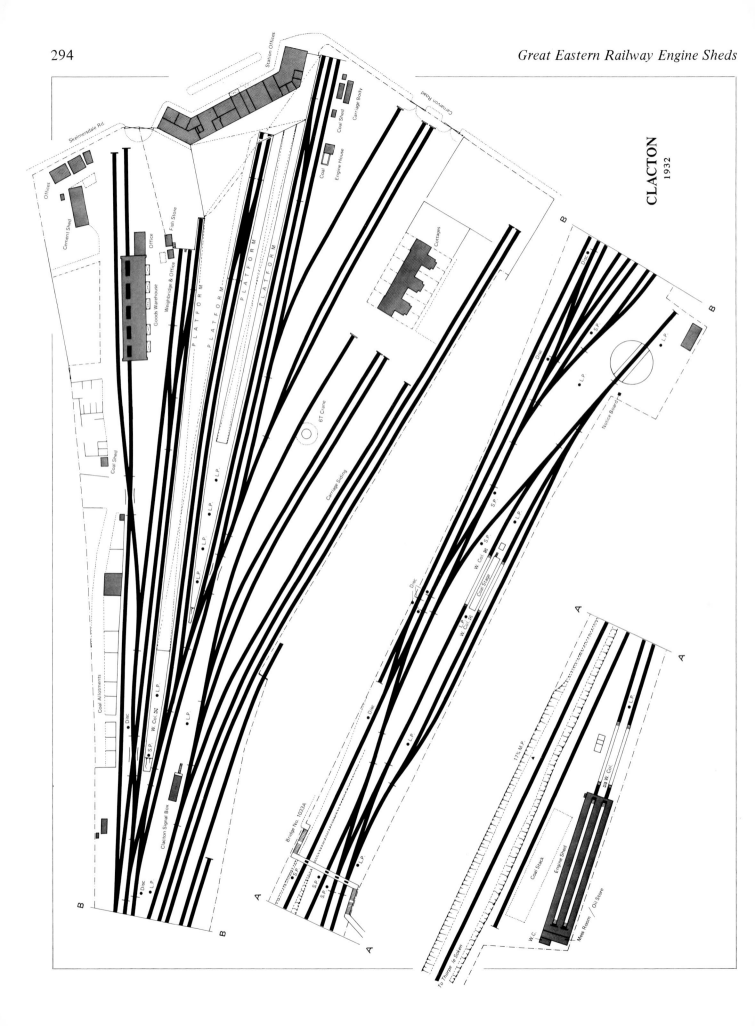

CLACTON
1932

Station Offices

Skelmersdale Rd

Carnarvon Road

Offices

Cement Shed

Office

Goods Warehouse

Weighbridge & Office

Fish Store

Coal Shed

Coal Shed

Coal

Engine House

Coal Shed

Carriage Body

Cottages

Coal Allotments

Clacton Signal Box

PLATFORM

PLATFORM

PLATFORM

PLATFORM

6T Crane

Carriage Siding

Disc

S.P.

W. Col.

L.P.

L.P.

L.P.

L.P.

L.P.

L.P.

L.P.

L.P.

Disc

Disc

Disc

S.P.

S.P.

L.P.

L.P.

W. Col.

W. Col.

Coal Stage

Notice Board

Disc

Disc

L.P.

L.P.

Bridge No. 1033A

S.P.

S.P.

S.P.

L.P.

A

A

B

B

B

B

17¾ M.P.

To Thorpe le Soken

Coal Stack

Engine Shed

W. Col.

W.C.

Mess Room / Oil Store

A

A

The *LNER Magazine* of 1928 contains an unexpected insight into the origins of the new Clacton engine shed: "As more powerful engines are now required for working the Clacton-on-Sea services, it has been necessary to provide at Clacton a turntable larger than that previously used. Improvements have also been made in the locomotive accommodation, which was much needed. New engine pits, water columns, and water tank have been provided and the disused Carriage Paint Shop at Felixstowe is to be removed to Clacton and utilised as an engine shed." Whether this transfer took place is unclear — the Clacton building was of only two roads but was indeed primitive enough to constitute a fair replica of the paint shop. Two years later the magazine makes reference to it as a 'new shed': "The work of reconstruction commenced in December 1928, and was completed in December, 1929. The scheme of new work comprised the erection of entirely new station buildings and the complete demolition of the old brick and wood structure, re-alignment of terminal passenger lines and platforms, re-arrangement and lengthening of existing goods sidings to provide additional cartage facilities, three additional sidings for locomotives, a new engine shed, engine pits and coaling stage, replacement of the old 50-ft diameter turntable with one of 60 ft diameter, erection of cast-iron water tank of 30,000 gallons capacity, and erection of a steel footbridge over the main line and engine sidings in order to abolish the old footpath level crossing." *W. A. Camwell*

it had a capacity of 2,500 gallons/hour and was one of a batch of nine ordered for the GE section.

From the foregoing it is reasonably clear that Clacton was not an easy place to work; despite primitive conditions it was concerned with quite smartly timed workings to London, business trains with an inconveniently vocal clientele as well as excursion and local traffic. In 1914 it was perhaps the main prize in Colchester's complex fiefdom, seven sets of men aided by a single coalman on night work.

Since at least the early 1930s engines outstationed at Clacton appear to have been main line passenger types, 4–4–0s and 4–6–0s leaving for London, the odd 2–4–2Ts pottering about the Tendring Hundred, Thorpe-le-Soken, St. Botolphs and so on. 'Clauds' and 'B12s' were for many years prominent. The commuter (business) trains ensured a constant pressure on both the LNER and BR (in social terms they were perhaps roughly equivalent to the Brighton line) to update services; indeed electrification demands arose at least as early as the 1930s. 'B17' 4–6–0s were thus sent to Clacton; in the late 1950s Nos. 61650 *Grimsby Town*, 61651 *Derby County*, 61662 *Manchester United* and 61666 *Nottingham Forest* were all there (outbased from Colchester), running up to Liverpool Street in the morning, returning to Clacton, followed by another Liverpool Street run and returning to Clacton in the evening. They were thus out all day, with coaling, repairs, etc. conducted mainly at night. The big 4–6–0s had originally supplemented the 'B12s' and 4–4–0s, as noted in the *Railway Observer*

during 1937: 'Clacton-on-Sea — 5 engines — B12 Nos. 8513, 8538, B12/3 Nos. 8518, 8576, D15 No. 8813. This stock is augmented as required at holiday periods by class B12 or B17 engines from Colchester. The shed also deals with numerous excursion engines during the summer.'

By 1954 Clacton's allocation was reported as seven 'B17' 4–6–0s with a single 'J69' 0–6–0T. On dieselisation of the Norwich

services in 1958, Britannia Pacifics made possible an acceleration of the business trains, lauded as 'Fast and Cheap by Britannia to Town'. Coaling of them was avoided as far as possible and turning the 4–6–2s must have been an exceedingly delicate operation, with less than two feet to spare on the 60 ft 'table.

Among the earliest large-scale BR electrification projects, the Clacton/Walton branches went over to EMU operation in March 1959,

J15 0–6–0 No. 7558 at Clacton in August 1932.   *Collection P. W. Swinger*

though business trains and excursions remained locomotive (increasingly diesel) hauled. The old shed, 'closing to steam' on 13th April 1959, was in fact extended, in modern style, to house the new multiple units and a 'temporary engine shed' erected in the yard for the diminishing numbers of steam locomotives employed. Diesels, Brush Type 2s in the main, seem to have ousted steam before full electric working began beyond Colchester to London in 1962, and yet another Great Eastern depot had 'faded away'. The alterations to Clacton shed (which for its size received more than its fair share over the years) were first planned in July 1956 and reported thus in the *Railway Magazine* of June 1959:

'In addition, the steam locomotive shed at Clacton has been converted into a temporary inspection and maintenance depot for electric rolling stock and a carriage washing plant is to be installed. Temporary shed accommodation for steam locomotives and two small buildings for staff accommodation, also have been built at Clacton.'

Clacton in 1939. Great Eastern 4—4—0s and 4—6—0s worked the best services, which developed a tradition of up-to-date express power. This culminated in 'Britannia' haulage in the 1950s and even trials with a 'Clan' — 72009 *Clan Stewart* from Kingmoor worked a number of turns in late 1958 including the 'Essex Coast Express' but made no great impression. *Collection John Hooper*

The GE section carried on a noble tradition of letting nothing go to waste and the timber-built shed (whether it owed much to the Felixstowe paint shop or no) was extended to house EMUs. A 'temporary shed' for surviving steam locos was erected but the multiple unit depot fashioned from the steam shed long outlasted the temporary nature envisaged in a *Railway Magazine* report of June 1957: "Clacton Branch Electrification Progress — Civil engineering work in preparation for the electrification of the line from Colchester to Clacton-on-Sea and Walton-on-the-Naze is progressing. The electrification is due for completion next year and is to be carried out on the new high-voltage a.c. system for the immediate purpose of testing new multiple-unit electric trains in the local services and of trying out certain new techniques. At a later stage there will be a link-up with the extension of electrification from Chelmsford to Ipswich. The engineering work involves the rebuilding of 21 bridges, the cutting back of station awnings, alterations to the track layout of seven stations, provision of load gauges and notices at level crossings, lengthening of sidings at Colchester and Walton, and the provision of an additional siding at Clacton. The steam locomotive shed at Clacton is to be adapted as a temporary inspection and maintenance depot for electric rolling stock, and alternative accommodation for steam locomotives and staff will be provided. Track slewing and re-positioning of points to make room for the erection of the overhead line equipment is yet to be carried out at Colchester, Hythe Junction, Wivenhoe, Great Bentley, Thorpe-le-Soken, Clacton and Walton. At Thorpe-le-Soken Station the centre track is to be converted for two-way working to allow trains stopped for division to be by-passed by non-stop services. Extensive drainage work has been completed at Thorpe-le-Soken, where the Holland Brook has been diverted to a new course so that the track embankments could be strengthened. Of the 21 bridges to be altered, 16 have to be raised to provide the necessary clearance for the overhead wiring, and the parapets of all are to be raised to conform with statutory regulations."   *W. T. Stubbs*

Walton started life contemporaneously with the shed at Clacton — a single road shed for the 'branch' engine and a turntable and sidings for locos off excursion workings. Walton never developed like Clacton and of all (English) railways the Great Eastern was surely the victim of class; it lacked economic 'clout' and was bullied by establishments as ancient as Cambridge and as *nouveau* as Frinton and Walton. It did more than most for the workers, of East London, and still made little money out of it.
National Railway Museum

WALTON

Terminus of an early and somewhat bold little venture, Walton on the Naze was considered deserving of engine shed and turntable from opening in 1867. The shed had only one road, a brick building on the north side of the station, designed originally and generously for a single locomotive outstationed from Colchester. Problems became manifest within a short time and the water supply was 'cut off' on 26th November 1868. A month later it was 'arranged with the foreman at Ipswich to supply the engine there with a travelling Tank by which the water would be conveyed from Weeley to Walton . . . Quality is not good at Walton and Mr. Johnson therefore recommends to take the future supplies from Weeley. The Engineer is arranging for a larger tank to replace the temporary one which is at present in use at Weeley. Resolved, that the supply be discontinued at Walton, and Station supply be collected from the roof. Water for Engines to be carried in a Tank from Weeley.'

Walton, of course, was long a destination for excursion traffic etc. and the yard could accordingly become quite congested. Its own work seems to have been much more restricted, a couple of tanks ('F3' and similar in the 1930s) engaged on the local service to Thorpe-le-Soken, etc. There were only seven men based there in 1914, a driver and two acting drivers with four acting firemen. The most junior of the latter group would have spent the greater part of his time loading ashes, cleaning fires and so on. Towards the end Walton was using an 'N7' 0-6-2T or perhaps a 'Gobbler' and boasted three sets of men.

The Walton turntable 'only 45 ft 6 ins . . . including extension rails'. Improvements, as at many of these GE sites, had to await a broader-based, LNER investment programme.
National Railway Museum

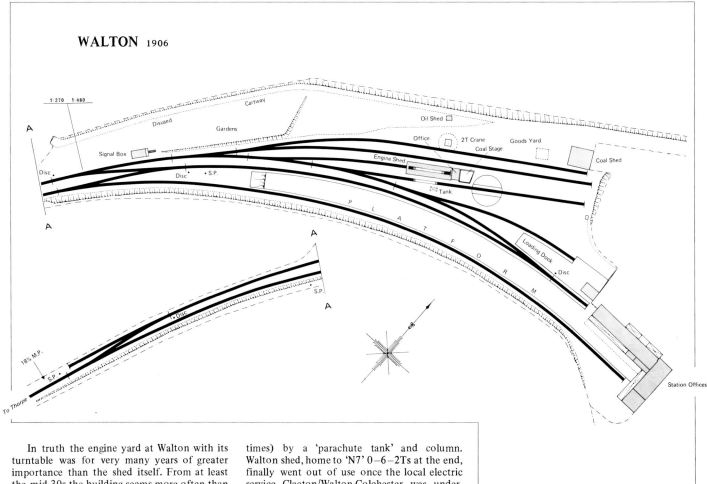

WALTON 1906

In truth the engine yard at Walton with its turntable was for very many years of greater importance than the shed itself. From at least the mid-30s the building seems more often than not to have housed various items of stock leading one contemporary correspondent (having just paid a visit) to describe it as 'disused'. The building, nevertheless, remained officially available for locomotive use, discreetly crumbling away with the minimum repair work necessary to forestall actual collapse. It was the turntable which occupied the authorities:

'LNER Locomotive Committee 21st June 1938 – The engine turntable at Walton-on-Naze which is 38 years old, is only 45′ 6″ in diameter including extension rails, and that consequently large engines overhang the table and allow only a small clearance of the adjoining sidings. The Ministry of Transport have intimated that, pending the provision of a large table on another site, engines which overhang the existing table should not be turned when the adjoining sidings are occupied by vehicles.

'There is a stock of serviceable Tables, 55′ in diameter including extension rails, which it is proposed to put down on a site adjacent to the existing turntable. This would accommodate all engines now working to Walton. Approved, the £1,469 needed.'

This turntable duly appeared on the existing lengthy spur, off the old 45 ft unit, coming into traffic with only minimum disruption. The old 'table is said to have been cut up and the foundations buried. The travelling tanks from Weeley, if ever they entered traffic, would have been rendered unnecessary by a new tank outside the shed. This had appeared, certainly by 1906, to be replaced (apparently in LNER times) by a 'parachute tank' and column. Walton shed, home to 'N7' 0–6–2Ts at the end, finally went out of use once the local electric service Clacton/Walton–Colchester was underway around 1960.

BR standard engines at Walton; on the GE section their versatility was seen at its best. Pre-Nationalisation (let alone pre-Grouping) prejudice was a minor factor and a number of key personnel were favourable disposed to the new engines.   *H. N. James*

The shed on 28th March 1937. Walton 2−4−2Ts, 'Crystal Palace' tanks in the 1920s, worked mainly to Thorpe le Soken. This local train would connect with a Clacton-Colchester service with the trains sometimes joined. The Walton engine then returned light.   *W. A. Camwell*

61611 *Raynham Hall* at Walton on 17th April 1949. These engines were only classified 4MT by BR and in theory the '76000' standard moguls could be directly substituted.   *T. J. Edgington*

With the development of railcar and electric services, N7 0—6—2Ts became available for work elsewhere and were in use on the Walton branch in the last years.

Dr. I. C. Allen

The sleepy branch line character was transformed on excursion days; several engines would require turning, some extra coal would be judged necessary and all made ready for the evening return trips. It also inevitably meant a motley collection of engines; in August 1954 B1 4−6−0 No. 61302, J15 0−6−0 No. 65475, an Ivatt 2MT mogul and B17 4−6−0 No. 61667 *Bradford* had all been summoned up.

D. Clayton

Walton on 2nd September 1960. The 'wires were up' but the extra coal stocks would indicate that steam was still around, on Saturdays at least. This would have been the last year that it was so.

W. T. Stubbs

The 'back ends' of country market towns could be unattractive places and the meanness of the Sudbury shed matched its surroundings, particularly in the rain.

W. A. Camwell

SUDBURY

Sudbury was akin to Braintree, a single road shed, left tucked away in a goods yard when the original terminus was abandoned. The line up from Marks Tey, an outpost of the Eastern Union Railway, had opened in 1849. The old station was turned over entirely to goods work in 1865, a new station opening to the west in August of that year (on 30th the Paving Commissioners complained of 'the incomplete state of the station') and the shed remained on its original site close by the mean buildings fronting King Street.

Little is known for certain of the shed's history. It is presumed to have opened with the line in 1849 but the earliest available plans showing it in operation date from 1876. Brick-built in a squat, distinctively unattractive style, it bore a flat, unventilated roof leading to suggestions that it was intended at first for carriages. It is not as yet possible to enlarge

Sudbury at the rear in 1939. These squat buildings were entirely unsuited for the stabling of steam locomotives, and the night man especially had a lonely and claustrophobic existence. The shed lay in a neglected yard, innocuous, if a bit shabby, but unlit and isolated, hedged in by unfamiliar and disturbing shapes by night.   *Peter Proud*

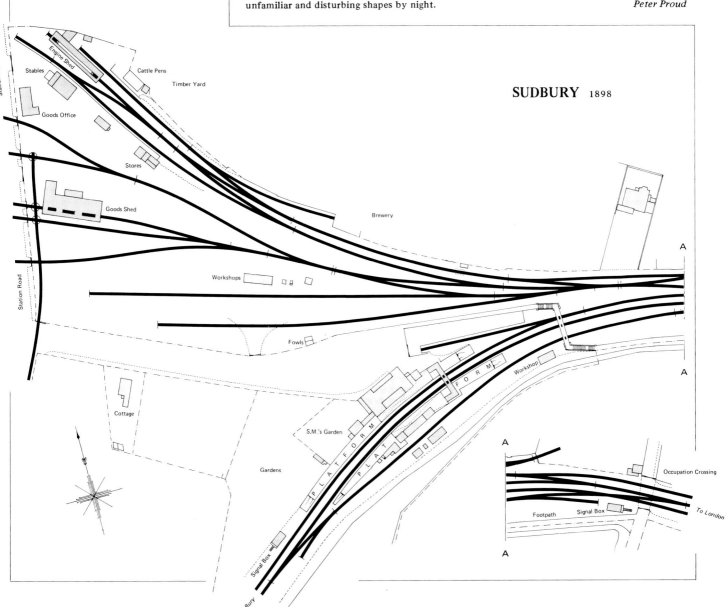

SUDBURY 1898

The shed was taken down at some time, perhaps around 1950, though the mess remained, suitably sealed against the weather, and attention to locomotives continued precisely as before (note the outdoor fitting arrangements). This was a Sunday in the mid-1950s, the two engines, C12 No. 67367 and E4 No. 62786, ready to leave within minutes of each other. One would set off at about 6.30 for Cambridge, the other at 6.35 for a Sudbury-Colchester-Cambridge-Colchester-Sudbury job.

Dr. I. C. Allen

upon this fascinating notion, or its obvious corollary – what form might the original engine shed accommodation have taken?

On a restricted site with extremely limited facilities (the little siding space available was normally occupied by coal wagons), Sudbury throughout GE days and until the late 1930s, was an outstation of Colchester, part indeed of the Ipswich District. No less than ten men were employed by 1914, working with tanks, 2–4–2Ts etc. on local passenger trains and with 0–6–0s on a still prosperous agricultural goods traffic. The five crews were made up of three full drivers, an acting driver, two firemen and four acting firemen. Three engines were outstationed in the early 'thirties, two 'F3' 2–4–2Ts and a 'J15' 0–6–0, the tanks in use in 1937 being Nos. 8064 and 8066. By 1939, with the dissolution of the Ipswich District, Sudbury found itself under Bury St. Edmunds in the Cambridge District, with two engines the normal complement. In the early 1950s 'E4' 2–4–0s from Cambridge were in use, Nos. 62791 and 62794, with 62784 spare, and in 1954 the *Railway Observer* noted under Sudbury: 'Sub to 31E Bury St. Edmunds 1 J15. Also, 1 E4 or J15 from 31A Cambridge usually remains overnight'.

What remained of the shed appears to have closed about 1959. On 1st January that year diesel sets were introduced on the Colchester-Cambridge line though steam locos might well have continued to turn up on goods for a period.

Sudbury, for much of the Great Eastern period, was part of the Ipswich District. LNER reorganisations meant it passed to Cambridge though, in a sense, it was 'returning home'. There is no doubt from the 1866-67 notebooks of George Macallan, the Cambridge DLS, that he was responsible for the Sudbury engines. Examples from 1866 include: No. 306 (Sinclair Z 2–4–0) sent to Sudbury on 6th March, EUR 2–2–2 No. 261 received from there on 19th April, 0–6–0 No. 1570 repaired at Sudbury on 26th May, Sinclair Y 2–4–0 No. 357 sent to Sudbury in place of 1570 on 2nd August and Z 2–4–0 No. 302 on a Sudbury trial trip on 25th August. On 23rd and 24th August 1866 Macallan attended a conference at Stratford on Sudbury engines from which it would seem that the main job was the heavy 2.5 p.m. Cambridge-Colchester goods/mixed train. As a result of the conference train services were cut and only one Sudbury engine was to be kept in steam. *Dr. I. C. Allen*

It was the odd habit in GE Section country areas to stable the new railcars as much after the fashion of steam locos as could be arranged. Hence this late 1950s contrast.
Dr. I. C. Allen

It is hard to use such terms as 'abandoned' or 'derelict', for the
'shed' had looked like this for years. More or less the end at
Sudbury, 31st August 1960.   *W. T. Stubbs*

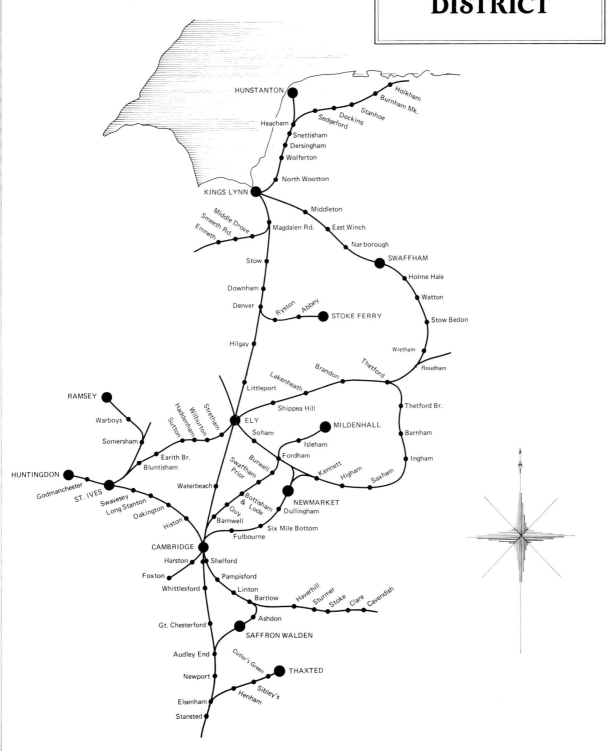

CAMBRIDGE LOCOMOTIVE DISTRICT

Cambridge station and shed in long-distant days. The sweeping curve within the confines of the station represents the (remains at least) of the old ('and troublesome') Newmarket curve, realigned to the north in 1896.

Collection Michael Brooks

The sequence of photography beginning on these pages has a quality somehow of unreality – frozen without people. Yet the detail holds endless fascination – the regular debris piles opposite and the individually attended look of every item of stock. *Collection Michael Brooks*

CAMBRIDGE

The Eastern Counties Railway opened its Cambridge station in 1845, making quite generous provision for locomotives more or less from the first. ECR plans of the period 1847-1848 show two separate sheds, a two road 'Engine House' facing the station, on the east side of the line, and a fine, four-road building, capable of housing twelve locos, on the west. This stood slightly to the north, backing onto the station yard. It was equipped with turntable and coke stage, with a single road carriage shed squeezed in nearby. In true GER tradition this remained the basis of the locomotive depot through to the end of steam. The two-road shed, in all likelihood, preceded its larger companion, representing the initial provision of 1845 and subsequently disappearing as the station, sidings etc. were expanded. The origins of the larger shed lay in an ECR minute of 9th April 1846: 'Tenders read for the erection of an Engine Shed at Cambridge and for a station at Ingatestone . . . Resolved, that the Tender of Mr. Peto for the Cambridge Engine Shed at the sum of £5940 0 0 . . . be accepted.'

The two-road Cambridge 'Engine House' with its tank and 'Coke Platform' must have survived a rearrangement completed in November 1863: 'New Passenger Station at Cambridge with Up and Down Platform [was] opened for Traffic on 16th instant.' Two years later, in 1865, with the arrival in prospect both of the

Midland and the Great Northern, the GER deliberated upon the facilities to be afforded the interlopers: 2nd August 1865: 'Accommodation to be offered the Great Northern Company (Platform office etc.) . . . together with an Engine House for not less than 2 Engines.'

'Midland Company Requirements: These will necessitate the removal of the *Great Eastern Locomotive Shed* [authors' italics] the making of another Passenger Platform . . . and an Engine Shed for 4 Locomotives. As in the case of the Great Northern Company the other goods warehouse now occupied by the Great Eastern Company will be made available.' Later, at the end of August, the Traffic Committee resolved that 'For the Passenger Traffic a new Passenger Dock and Platform to be made on the site of the existing Locomotive Shed with siding accommodation for 20 vehicles. A separate Locomotive Engine Shed for Four Engines to be provided at the North end of the Station.' The GE shed to be 'removed' is assumed, of course, to have been the two-road 'Engine House' of the 1840s. Other than the bare fact of its eventual removal, however, the precise fate of the building remains unclear. MR locos from their arrival in 1866 were housed (with a deal of reluctance on both sides) at the main GE shed whilst a separate establishment was eventually erected for the GN. Whatever precisely befell the 'Great Eastern Locomotive Shed', it had certainly disappeared by about 1880, the early ECR four-road shed

having for long years formed the great part of the locomotive depot.

In August 1868 the GE were arranging for tenders regarding a 45 ft turntable 'for the GN traffic', but any last hopes the Midland may have cherished for its own shed seem to have ended following a visit on 11th and 12th September: 'New Goods Shed and Engine House accommodation. It was not considered desirable to go on with [this] and the Midland demands be limited to what accommodation can now be afforded them.' As already noted, this took the form of some limited stabling room in the GE's own, four-road shed. The Great Northern shed was eventually completed in 1869 but stood to the south of the main station: '5th May 1869 (Engine Shed for Great Northern Railway) . . . now complete and ready for their occupation.' From about this time the Great Eastern's straight shed assumes a greater clarity, emerging from a haze of tantalisingly imprecise references. Platform extensions, including double bays at each end, had drawn the shed within the confines of the station itself, forcing the removal of the original turntable and coal stage to a site in the northern part of the yard. The building had acquired a row of offices, workshops, etc. on the west side by about 1880, along with a plethora of assorted buildings, shops, huts and shacks devoted to a comprehensive range of repairs and reflecting absolutely the GE predisposition to the Dickensian. Even by this early date overcrowding was chronic – George Macallan, Cambridge District

The north end at Cambridge (top) with a trace of some of the short stub sidings (seven in all, on an imperfectly drawn Ordnance plan of 1901) which were placed on the west side. Their purpose is unclear; almost every one was too short for engines, and sidings had to be both foreshortened and diverted because of them. The water tank, seen to better effect in the lower view, bears some considerable resemblance to the equally ancient Ipswich example (see elsewhere) and was indeed of a type familiar at a number of early GE sites.
Collection Michael Brooks

Engine disposal at Cambridge for years took place at the north end of the yard, an endlessly laborious sequence of dumping and loading waste material, from the noxious to the merely unpleasant. Labouring conditions on the Great Eastern remained hard — 'cruel and hard'. The very poverty of the working methods are a lingering theme, difficult to banish from the mind; no other company would service a comparable fleet of engines in this fashion and all had long developed their own variation on the London North Western 'coal hole'. The concept of gravity, and how it might be employed to ease the task of ash and coal handling, was not unknown to the GE — the problem of paying for it was.   *Collection Michael Brooks*

Cambridge in the summer of 1911.   *Collection Michael Brooks*

Photograph dated 13th August 1911 and labelled 'Cambridge: from roof of engine cab in yard at end of platform looking towards Newmarket'.

Collection Michael Brooks

'From back of tender in loco yard looking towards office'. *Collection Michael Brooks*

Locomotive Superintendent, had *fourteen* years earlier been bemoaning 'the want of room'. The MR, for instance, had taken to stabling five engines of their own instead of the original three and, although Derby contemplated building a shed of their own in the 1890s, it never got beyond a variety of proposals, estimates, etc. The Midland indeed continued until grouping to pay the GE 6d for every tank of loco water taken.

The Great Eastern shed was so closely situated within the station precincts that members of the public habitually used the yard as some kind of short cut. In October 1867 these activities were made known and it was ordered that fences be put up, 'it being desirable to keep the Locomotive Yard more private than it is at present.' In January 1878 a proposal arose for a much needed 'footpath for Locomotive Workmen' at the depot. There were two possibilities, one priced at £50, the other at £25 and it is not necessary to record which alternative was chosen.

Principal shed of a main GE District, the Cambridge complement stood soon at over 100 locomotives. An inspector, G. Dorrington (whose responsibilities included 'testing for promotion, eyesight etc.'), rather than a foreman, was in charge of the footplate crews — 101 drivers (31 acting) and 89 firemen (47 acting) around the Great War period. The foreman fitter at that time had some 70 staff for locomotive maintenance and repairs, other than boiler work which was the responsibility of a foreman boilermaker. Wagon repairs, under a leading carpenter, were also carried out at Cambridge. Another foreman, A. Wilson, was charged with day to day affairs and over 150 men at Lynn, a duty considered onerous enough for a junior clerk 'to assist Wilson in

0–6–0T No. 11. Repair work at Cambridge bore many similarities to Ipswich, both a living rebuttal to any notions of planned servicing, purpose building, 'concentration' and the rest. This appears to be the 'repair shops' in the yard near to Devonshire Road, the lofty extension (the whole building would be timber framed and slightly shaky, as at Ipswich) accommodating the shear-legs. *Collection W. G. Rear*

office work'. A further 70 footplatemen were based at no less than eleven outstations, all under a 'Driver in Charge': Ely, Huntingdon, Saffron Walden, Newmarket, Mildenhall, St. Ives, Ramsey, Thaxted, Hunstanton, Swaffham and Stoke Ferry.

Water at Cambridge was to prove troublesome over the years; it was not of the highest quality and the amount abstracted fell critically close to that consumed each day. Nearly

£3,000 was accordingly expended in 1900 on pipes from Chesterton Junction (some distance to the north) to a new tank in the depot. This was to have been of 30,000 gallons capacity but in April the company 'considered it wiser' to have a tank of 50,000 gallons, accordingly approved at an additional cost of £628. The new supply was not wholly successful and in March 1902 complaints were made that the Chesterton Junction well was 'inadequate' and that new pumps etc. were required. Quality difficulties remained in addition to the problems regarding supply and were not really resolved until LNER days. By this period conditions – inadequate machinery, dilapidation, overcrowding – had deteriorated to a truly appalling degree. It is a measure of the privation endured at Cambridge that the GE directors were actually moved to order improvements – they paid a visit on 15th June 1907 which caused such concern that Holden was charged at once with producing remedial plans, drawings, etc. His proposals totalled some £4,350, '£2175 to Capital Account and £2175 to Revenue'. It was received thus: 'It was felt that there was an imperative necessity for some improvement to be made. The plan prepared by Mr. Holden was examined and it was felt that while the arrangements proposed therein would be sufficient for present requirements it was desirable that room should be left for future extension. Mr. Holden will therefore reconsider the matter from this point of view and the whole question will be brought up before the Locomotive Committee.' There is no mention of further action for several years.

The shed as first built appears to have had some kind of pitched roof arrangement and the GER improvements, when at last they materialised, mainly comprised a new roof. The tender of A. Coe, £1,479 0s 0d for a 'New Roof over

The Great Eastern lacked much in terms of prestige and wealth. It wanted for little, however, in innovation and a readiness to adapt. These qualities in part sprang from its less than secure financial base, a situation which prompted less complacency than was exhibited, perhaps, in concerns generally regarded as more successful. Oil fuelling was a technique pioneered (on any scale at least) on the GER and partly through the 'experimental' nature of the work and partly through short money, the arrangements invariably contrived to appear a trifle 'homespun'. This is neither critique nor accolade, but oil fuelling would never have looked like this, one is convinced, on, say, the Great Western.   *Collection W. G. Rear*

Tanks at Cambridge. The buildings are assumed to be the corrugated iron 'shops' and the 2–4–0 is of note. The GER was 'quite fond of this lark', though the reason at Cambridge is unknown.
                                                                                                                    Collection W. G. Rear

'From Hills Road signal box looking north', Cambridge appeared like this on 13th August 1911. Cambridge, like Oxford, was cosmopolitan in company terms and the text relates to Great Eastern concern at the arrival of the Midland and the Great Northern. The latter's shed lay to the right (top) whilst the LNWR also had a shed on the London side of the bridge, its smoke vents visible in the lower view. *Collection Michael Brooks*

The LNWR shed was probably built by or on behalf of the GER, for the buildings round about, including the GNR shed and goods sheds, beyond the road bridge, had a similar look about them. The LNWR shed was briefly described in *LMS Engine Sheds Vol. 1* (Wild Swan) but it is doubtful now if the building itself was used to a great extent. All photographs show its doors firmly closed, with stock in the yard and evidence of engine servicing only on the turntable approach. The LMS rearranged matters so that all necessary coaling could take place at Bletchley and other details could be dealt with at the ex-GER shed from about 1935. Coaling of LMS engines working into Cambridge was taken over by the LNER, with the benefit of mechanical plant, during the war, saving labour at Bletchley.   *Collection Michael Brooks*

The LNWR line (and signal box) into Cambridge, August 1911.   *Collection Michael Brooks*

'From small signal post with three goods arms near Hills Road bridge looking towards station'.   *Collection Michael Brooks*

Old Engine Shed', was accepted on 5th June 1913 and the familiar Cambridge northlight pattern covering is assumed to date from shortly afterwards. Opportunity was taken to construct a further three roads on the west side; such action temporarily secured the immediate accommodation problem and engines could now be attended to in relatively civilised conditions. The problem by this time was how to get them there; the depot was still grotesquely crowded and the yard layout primitive in the extreme. The turntable and coal stage positions had been altered again since the 1880s, the former enlarged to 55 ft by 1918, but the latter comprising no more than a simple open platform. Up to seven spur sidings had been provided

off the 'table in earlier years but these disappeared as yard alterations inexorably progressed.

Repair work had grown up in ludicrously haphazard fashion over the years and by 1923 operated from a series of (often partly derelict) buildings ranging from stores and a machine shop tucked in the south-west corner, through smiths and carpenters premises strung out in a long line of hovels merging with what was grandly termed the 'Locomotive Shops'. This was again a peculiarly linear feature, developed piecemeal over the years within the strict constraints of the site. These premises had originated long years before as a small timber shack containing the shear-legs, and by 1923

engines were being repaired at the rate of 75 a year, an astonishing and most praiseworthy figure carried out to high standards amidst exacting surroundings. Siding room, pits, the most trifling operational convenience and the simplest aids to working comfort were largely absent from Cambridge. On 24th May 1918 the Traffic Committee were mortified to learn that at the Cambridge coal stage 'men have no protection from the weather' and they had 'sent in a petition asking for a covering'. £454 was approved to remedy this state of affairs but less easily corrected problems came to notice in April 1922: 'Our accommodation for the manhandling of engines at Cambridge is inadequate.' £464 was made available for additional pits etc. to avoid engines lighting up all over the yard and 'obviate the need for preparing engines at Tennyson Field Siding (adjoining Tennyson Road, and an extensive coal stacking area) which has resulted in applications from enginemen for additional time to be allowed when preparing engines there.'

The LNER looked understandably askance at this rambling assemblage and Cambridge was a priority in the wholescale rearrangement and updating of locomotive affairs on the GE section. It needed transformation into a proper 'District' depot, with modern repair facilities. Despite heroic work by staff over many decades it was impossible to question Vincent Raven's verdict, 'that means be taken early' to close down such 'subsidiary works'; Raven's examination of the various running departments proved fatal for the old GE organisation and its outstation shops. Shortcomings had become apparent as early as 1874 when a 'screw cutting Tap 12″ Lathe and a planing machine' were urgently ordered for the depot, £210 and £100 respectively. Doubtless the LNER found them still in use in 1923. A degree of centralism was an inevitable product both of the Grouping and the subsequent Depression, reflecting economic and industrial trends in general. Thus it was in 1930 that the LNER set about the re-ordering of Cambridge. On 25th September the Locomotive Committee heard that the depot, responsible for 111 locomotives, 'fell short of requirements' and that 'in the interests of economy and efficiency the engine shed should be enlarged, in accordance with plan No. 16038'. Accompanying the long vanished document was a series of proposals:

(1) Extension of Loco Shed for a length of 200 feet to enable 49 Engines to be accommodated under cover
(2) New combined oil and general stores, mess and offices necessitated by the altered layout
(3) An automatic coaling plant, 200 tons capacity, divided into two compartments in the ratio 2:1
(4) Hot water washing out plant
(5) Two new parallel ashpits 150 ft long. Two new preparation pits 150 ft and 7 new preparation pits each 50 ft long.
(6) 70 ft turntable, replacing one 55 ft in diameter [the replacement of this 'table had first arisen in October 1924, when its substitution by a redundant 52 ft unit from Kings Cross had been discussed. Costs had been estimated at £760 but it was decided that a 70 ft 'table could be provided for only an additional £40. Obviously no action was taken.]

Accommodation had grown up over long years at Cambridge and accordingly bore all the accretionary hallmarks. Posts, pipes, buckets, wooden and corrugated iron additions, and, of course, the coach body, had all appeared and survived, in December 1931, the rebuilding of the shed.
R. H. R. Garraway, courtesy A. Garraway

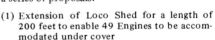

Boiler Foreman Running Foreman Running Foreman C&W. Foreman Running Foreman
King   Ross   Steel   Heavens   Rix
Foreman Fitter Ass. Dist. Loco'Supt. Dist. Loco'Supt. Chief Running Inspector
Beaumont R.H.R.Garraway C.H.M. Elwell Foreman Bailey Walpole

Cambridge Circa. 1925

Courtesy A. Garraway

The ancient Cambridge coal stage, 7th December 1931, its days numbered as the new mechanical coaler took shape elsewhere in the yard.
R. H. R. Garraway, courtesy A. Garraway

Shear-legs of various sorts (secondhand, no doubt) were necessary at Cambridge and stood in the open alongside the shed in the period following Raven's verdicts on the place as an 'outstation' and prior to the LNER provision of a covered 'lifting shop'. 7th December 1931.
R. H. R. Garraway, courtesy A. Garraway

R. H. R. Garraway was Assistant Locomotive Running Superintendent at Cambridge from 1924 to 1941; he was present during the LNER re-ordering of Cambridge depot and recorded much of the work as it took place. Above, the coaling plant is nearing completion, on 26th February 1932, along with modern LNER sand dispensers. Left is the lower portion of the plant the previous year, on 7th December 1931.

R. H. R. Garraway, courtesy A. Garraway

Work on the new stores and mess rooms, 1st March 1932. The top view is presumably from the new coaler and it is easy to overlook the shed beyond.
R. H. R. Garraway, courtesy A. Garraway

The new coaler on 30th August 1932. The shed lies, white, beyond with the blankly ugly lifting shop to the right.

R. H. R. Garraway, courtesy A. Garraway

The Cambridge ash pits on 24th August 1932.   *R. H. R. Garraway, courtesy A. Garraway*

(7) Electrically operated wheel drop to replace hand operated shear legs. [Electricity for running power machinery had been approved on 29th March 1928, cost £984] and a new building to accommodate

(8) An electric air compressor in the machine shop for blowing out super heater tubes

(9) Three new water columns, and alter the position of five existing

(10) A new 'Keystone' sand furnace with bunkers for dried and wet sand

(11) A cycle store

(12) New, improved layout for yard exit with more 'standage' space

(13) A footbridge at Devonshire Road into the depot.

This scheme accommodates 130 locos. The displacement of the CME's wagon repairing shops necessitated by the extension of the shed will result in the former GN shed being converted for their use. Estimated Cost £108 167.'

Approval of the whole was recommended subject to a satisfactory grant being obtained from the Government under the terms of the Development (Loans Guarantees and Grants) Act 1929. This measure was responsible for a number of engine shed renewals across the country in the 1930s.

Like the Norwich example, the Cambridge coaling plant was provided by Henry Lees & Co., their tender of £5,752 1s 4d being approved on 4th May 1931; following a hard war the firm was subsequently called in to carry out extensive repairs in the summer of 1946, totalling £2,515. A water softener was the only omission

The Cambridge plant in use on 30th August 1932. The great Stratford coaler (see Part One) was a considerable achievement though it came about only in the company's very last days. The (relative) financial good health of the LNER, together with government investment policy brought the benefits of mechanical plant out to the 'pudds' in East Anglia and at both Norwich and Cambridge concrete plants were put up. Their design was largely the responsibility of a small coterie of private specialist firms, in the days when a healthy home market was considered an essential springboard for foreign sales. Government grants to the railways were accordingly vital and a captive Empire market helped.

R. H. R. Garraway, courtesy A. Garraway

in the comprehensive 1930 project, though allocation was made in the 1939 programme for a unit to the value of £11,670, 'capacity 109 million gallons per annum.'

Like the other district sheds, Norwich, Ipswich, etc., Cambridge saw the full range of passenger and goods types. It was a prime appointment held in 1866 by one George Macallan. His diary notes have survived, skilfully summarised by Canon C. S. Bayes. "2–4–0s and singles predominated in the forty or so locos Macallan found on his arrival; by October 1869 no less than eight of the 'six-wheeled coupled Engines' were at Cambridge, only Stratford possessing more. They were working to Newmarket, London, Bury, Peterboro' and Ipswich".

The Cambridge post could pose certain 'political' difficulties, particularly in the early years when University sensibilities were at their height. Royal workings were also a worry and any shortcomings attracted the immediate scrutiny of the Board. With its variety of main line and branch work, Cambridge continued to house a varied complement, modern types and relative antiques, through to closure. 2–4–0s found continuing use and the last 'E4' was not withdrawn until 1959. 'B1s' and 'B17s' replaced many of the '1500s' and 'Clauds' and

Cambridge machine shop and new offices, 30th August 1932.

R. H. R. Garraway, courtesy A. Garraway

Silver Fox on the new Cambridge turntable. An unusual duty 'worked by Kings Cross A4s on Thursdays and Saturdays' (RCTS *History*) took the Pacifics to Cambridge on a regular basis, 'very popular and loaded heavily'.

R. H. R. Garraway, courtesy A. Garraway

A. H. Rees, District Locomotive Running
Superintendent at Cambridge, 1936.
R. H. R. Garraway, courtesy A. Garraway

R. H. R. Garraway, in 1936, Assistant Locomotive Running Superintendent, Cambridge,
1924-1941. A party of 'chiefs', including
Gresley, visited Cambridge before the
rebuilding and enquired of the ALRS his
opinion regarding the size of the new shed.
He ventured that it was difficult to show any
financial saving, simply on the *size* of the depot
and was told to design what he wanted for
efficient working within the constraints of the
site.

Courtesy A. Garraway

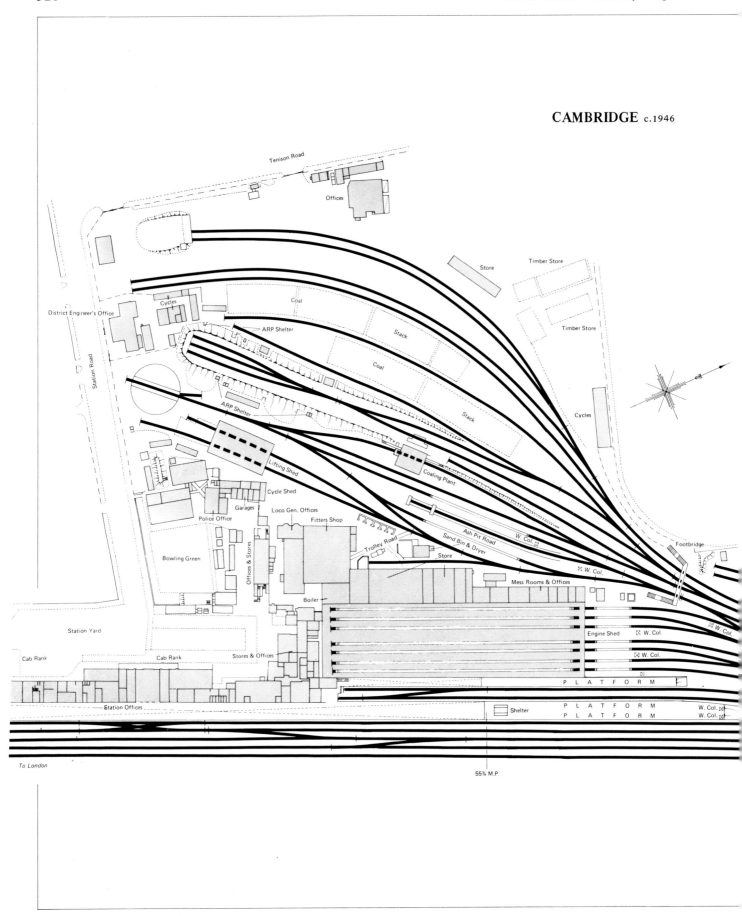

CAMBRIDGE c.1946

4-4-0 No. 7744 at Cambridge on 30th August 1934. Allocations are given as follows: May 1933: B12: 8511/2/4/20-2/6/7/30. B17: 2817-9. C1: 3297, 4402/4/30/41. C2: 3257/60. D13: 7779, 8012/5/6/21/3/8. D15: 8810-2/6/8/23/4/30/5/6/52/60/5/6/76/82/90/6/9. D16: 8783/4/7/95. E4: 7409/21/7/41/63/79/90/2/6. F3: 8044/60/3/82. F4: 7105/74, 7220. G4: 8139. J15: 7510/8/21/3/48/9/53/70/1, 7825/33-8/45/8/9/51/6/7/70/5/97, 7928/9. J17: 8179. J19: 8254/63-5/7-9/79/81. J66: 7287/91/8, 7300/2/7. J67: 7011, 7169, 7397-9, 7404/5. J69: 7162/93, 7271, 7372/88. K2: 4656. O4: 6204, 6498, 6506/20/7/93. Y3: 60/1, 87, 94. And in 1936: 60/1, 78, 87, 98, 2817-9, 3252/7/97, 4402/30/9/40, 4646/ 56, 6498, 6506/20/7/93, 7049/50, 7128/31/3/4/6/62/74/90/3, 7271/9/94/8, 7300/2/18/90, 7404/5/77/90, 7512/21/48/9/53/70/1, 7642, 7825/ 36/7/9/43/5/8/9/51/71/5/6/96/7, 7911, 8016/21/3/8/44/61/3/91, 8105/39, 8254/63-5/7/8/79/81, 8511/2/4/20-2/6/7/30, 8783/7/95, 8801/10/ 1/6/8/20/3/4/30/5/6/52/60/5/6/76/82/8/90/6/9, 07126.   *Collection Roger Simmonds*

The concentration of engines 'in steam' continued at the north end despite the complete reorganisation of the shed and yard and recalled pre-Great War practice.

Dr. I. C. Allen

2—4—0 No. 62794 at Cambridge.

H. N. James

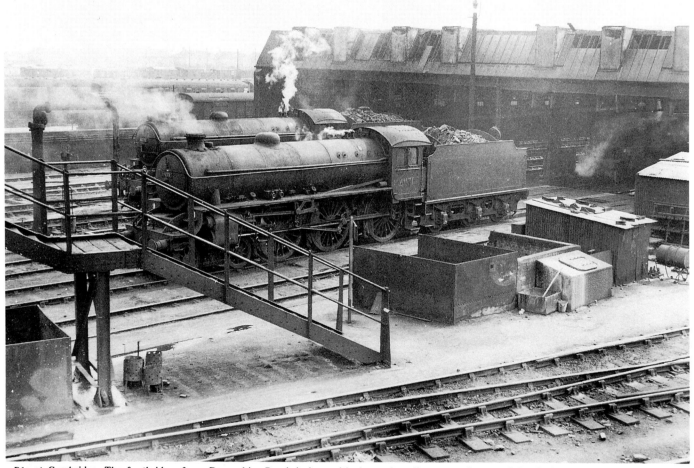

B1s at Cambridge. The footbridge, from Devonshire Road, in iron with sleeper boarding, was a feature of the shed and dated from the LNER rebuilding.

Dr. I. C. Allen

Cambridge was a locomotive centre of considerable import and the LNER improvements were made in recognition of this. The leaking column recalls the water problem at Cambridge, which came from some distance; the text notes the problems with the Chesterton Junction supply and from the 1930s water was taken from as far as Fulbourne, out on the Newmarket line. It was 'not marvellous' and caused endless problems. Ash disposal was accomplished through a sunken wagon road, an LNER exploitation of the gravity principle.   *Dr. I. C. Allen*

4–4–0 No. 6243 under the sand hopper on 4th April 1958.   *B. Hilton*

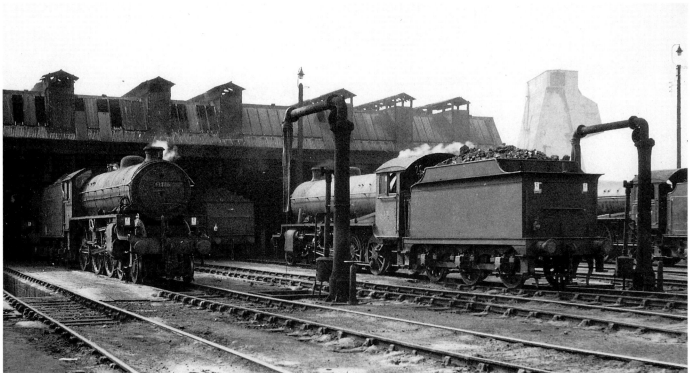

Cambridge in the 1950s.   *Dr. I. C. Allen*

The 4–6–0 *Royal Sovereign* carried on a long tradition of 'Royals' at Cambridge. No. 61671 was considered a wonderfully responsive engine (it received an almost unique level of attention) and 'would have steamed on house bricks'. For years past Cambridge had worked the 'Royal Clauds', in the 1930s 8783 and 8787; R. H. R. Garraway indeed arranged for the former to receive the last GE chimney, discovered languishing in a corner of Stratford works. It carried this until June 1939, when rebuilding work was necessary consequent upon hitting a hay lorry at Hilgay. There were three sets of 'Royal' men; they worked to Lynn and Kings Cross, "and if 'Royal' men were unavailable, the engines did not work".   *H. N. James*

J15 65478 lost inside the shed in the early 1950s. The smoke chutes at this time seem to have been in less than perfect condition.   *H. N. James*

'B1' 4–6–0s performed much of the work at Cambridge in latter years and were amongst the last engines at the shed. On 'the loss of the last steam passenger workings in 1960' most found their way to March.

Dr. I. C. Allen

Cambridge on 4th September 1960. The steam allocation had been reported reduced to only fifteen by late 1960, and effective closure from June 18th 1962. Last engines were transferred to March . . . "2–6–0s Nos. 43086, 43105, 43149 and 46400/65/6/9/94; 4–6–0s ('B1') Nos. 61286-7, 61300/71; and ex-GER 0–6–0s Nos. 65469, 65576, and 65582. A depot for diesel shunters and railcars still exists at Cambridge."

a succession of 'foreign' types characterised the period, 0–6–0s ex-NER and GNR passenger tanks and even LMS designs.

Passenger work on the wandering rural lines of the district was early on given over to diesels and the 1950 allocation is accordingly of some interest:

'B1' 4–6–0: 61121, 61285, 61286, 61287, 61300, 61301, 61302, 61333, 61334

'B2'/'B17' 4–6–0: 61617 *Ford Castle*, 61619 *Welbeck Abbey*, 61620 *Clumber*, 61622 *Alnwick Castle*, 61623 *Lambton Castle*, 61624 *Lumley Castle*, 61625 *Raby Castle*, 61627 *Aske Hall*, 61628 *Harewood House*, 61631 *Serlby Hall*, 61636 *Harlaxton Manor*, 61637 *Thorpe Hall*, 61638 *Melton Hall*, 61640 *Somerleyton Hall*, 61642 *Kilverstone Hall*, 61643 *Champion Lodge*, 61652 *Darlington*, 61653 *Huddersfield Town*, 61655 *Middlesbrough*, 61657 *Doncaster Rovers*, 61663 *Everton*, 61671 *Royal Sovereign*

'D16' 4–4–0: 62516, 62525, 62530, 62531, 62543, 62549, 62551, 62557, 62558, 62567, 62571, 62574, 62603, 62615, 62618

'E4' 2–4–0: 62781, 62783, 62784, 62785, 62788, 62794

'J10' 0–6–0: 64645, 64646, 64647, 64653, 64658, 64673

'J15' 0–6–0: 65356, 65391, 65405, 65425, 65438, 65451, 65457, 65461, 65474, 65474, 65477

'J17' 0–6–0: 65501, 65502, 65503, 65505, 65506, 65517, 65520, 65525, 65529, 65532, 65535, 65537, 65538, 65546, 65547, 65561, 65563, 65565, 65573, 75575, 65580, 65585, 65587, 65588, 65589

'F6' 2–4–2T: 67222
'C12' 4–4–2T: 67360, 67367, 67375, 67385
'J67/9' 0–6–0T: 63509, 68516, 68530, 68579, 68609
'J68' 0–6–0T: 68645

The diesel sets were looked after at a new depot, Coldham Lane, opened in 1958, steam working finally ceasing from Cambridge in June 1962. The shed was afterwards demolished and the site cleared, leaving an ugly brick-strewn wilderness.

Walter K. Whigham in the late 1950s, maintaining the tradition of visiting Pacifics.

R. Carpenter

King's Lynn on Saturday, 4th June 1938. The place was often simply 'Lynn' on the Great Eastern – officially it is said until 1911.

R. F. Roberts

King's Lynn on 15th May 1947. The roads were numbered 1-4 north to south, left to right in this photograph. Much of No. 1 road was taken up with coal and any engines standing upon it were generally for washing out. No. 2 was the coaling road with 3 and 4 for general purposes, 'fitting, storage and bedding of engines'.

H. C. Casserley

KING'S LYNN

The four-road shed at Lynn, through many years the main depot of a separate King's Lynn District, opened at some time prior to the early 1880s. There was at least one earlier shed, dating from the first years; this is believed to have been the two road building, some 100 ft x 27 ft close by the north side of the station, enlarged in 1871. Moreover, this building is closely associated with a variety of smaller brick structures, all of ancient aspect and with every indication of long, incremental growth. Most prominent amongst them was a substantial boiler house, and attached stores, workshops etc. dating from the late 1840s/early 1850s. All of the original and varied 'depot' was, of course, with GE economy incorporated into the later layout. On Great Eastern plans this early two-road building, entirely eclipsed by the generously proportioned later building is unequivocally labelled 'Loco Shed'.

The later shed at King's Lynn may well be contemporary with the new station of 1871 — traffic had grown prodigiously in the years before this and the GE had been rather put out by approaches from the Lynn and Sutton Bridge Railway. The Traffic Committee heard in January 1866 from a Mr. Eckersley of the Sutton Company that 'the line would open for Public Traffic on 1st February next'. The L & S intended to work the line themselves 'but it was not improbable that the Midlands might ulti-

mately work the line'. Mr. Eckersley went on to declare that engine stabling would be required, ' . . . Engine Shed for 2 Engines — If Great Eastern Railway cannot find accommodation the Lynn and Sutton Company will erect a Shed on their own account.' The GER had formulated a lengthy rejoinder by 14th February noting ruefully that 'the Lynn and Sutton will unfortunately be a competitor . . . for traffic now carried over our line to and from Peterboro'.' A number of variously restrictive terms and conditions were then laid down for the interloper (despite the L & S entitlement under their Act to the use of all GER facilities) although their sharing of the engine shed seemed on a more or less reasonable basis: 'Use of Engine House, Coke Stage, Turntable, Sidings and Water for two engines — Lynn and Sutton to find their own Engines.' The L & S reply to the whole arrangement was not enthusiastic, 'impossible to live under such a burden'. It thus appears Lynn and Sutton Bridge locos were accommodated separately from the first.

An improved water supply was arranged at Lynn in June 1867, 50,000 gallons a day from the Town Council, at £100 per year and much time was afterwards devoted to alterations attendant upon the new station. The four-road shed, which might well have grown out of these developments, was on a scale befitting a district headquarters. In GE terms, accommodation was positively lavish, whilst great kudos was attached to the post of (latterly) foreman at King's Lynn. The depot was intimately concerned with royal

train workings and the unthinkable consequences of any drastic operational failure must have made it a nerve-racking position. The royal train had to reverse at the station, requiring two 'royal' engines plus standbys, whilst the stock itself was housed opposite, in a 'Royal Train Shed', a covered single road some 350 ft in length. In February 1880 the whole establishment was described as 'Lynn Shops', an indication of its 'district' status. A list of 'Engines which do not run trains' (e.g. damaged beyond repair, etc.) included 'No. 910 . . . is a stationary boiler'. The shed was designed to accommodate a dozen engines and the allocation by 1885 stood at twenty-four.

In June 1892 there is a note 'Alterations to enable Engines to be moved from either of the shed roads without fouling the Goods Road, £360'. Tenuity indeed, this meagre reference might well suggest with its use of 'either' that the earlier two-road shed was still in use. In 1912 'the floor of the engine shed' was discovered to be 'in bad condition . . . to relay this with wood blocks laid end grain on a bed of concrete and grouted in with pitch is estimated to cost £400.' The shed, thus suitably refurbished, entered the Great War, at the end of which a proper coaling shelter was at last provided. For long years a simple low platform, narrow and hazardous, had sufficed but at the end of 1918 a somewhat elaborate canopy and stage etc. arose on the north side of the engine yard. Making use of redundant wrought iron and other items, it included a hut for the coal-

Engines at 'Lynn'. *Above:* 4−4−0 No. 0708 on 1st April 1902. *Below:* 2−4−0 No. 764 on 12th September 1910.   *K. Nunn/LCGB*

'The Royal Train Shed' narrowly avoided destruction in the First World War; a remarkable near miss on the Kaiser's relatives, the photograph is dated 19th January 1915. The *Daily Sketch* of 21st reported 'The Hole' as '7 ft deep, 17 ft wide . . . which was caused by a bomb 30 yards from the Royal Shelter at King's Lynn'. The King's Lynn 'Royal Shed' housed the royal train whilst the royal family were at Sandringham; it was afforded an extraordinary degree of attention — 'an engine was coupled to it most of the time, and continuously during the winter for steam heating purposes'.   *Charles Goodwin, courtesy Harry Ellis*

men and was positioned aside the most northerly of the four shed roads. This in itself was an inconvenience and its operation continued to rely on hand labour, the basis of coaling at King's Lynn until the end. '3rd October 1918. No protection from the weather is provided the men who engage in coaling engines at Kings Lynn . . . Recommended . . . immediately . . . in view of the approaching winter. £196.'

Before the dissolution of its district, Lynn would have been directly responsible for all the minor sheds in the area. On incorporation under Cambridge it was put in the charge of a locomotive foreman, responsible to the DLS at Cambridge and in the official hierarchical listings of 1914 the 'outstations' are separate. It would not have made sense, however, for day to day affairs at Stoke Ferry, Swaffham or Hunstanton, for instance, to be ordered from Cambridge and life at sites like these seems to have gone on much as before. Wisbech was given up to Peterborough though in truth its historical association was never wholly ended. Trams from Wisbech shed continued to turn up for repairs and it was worked as a King's Lynn sub-shed throughout LNER days. Swaffham duties in the early 'fifties were still worked partly by Lynn men though paperwork, returns etc. were forwarded to Norwich. King's Lynn must presumably have also seen some reduction in its capacity for repairs. Shear-legs had long been (and remained) in use on a road at the rear of the shed but despite the 1880 description, 'Lynn Shops', Raven, early in 1923, quite clearly considered it of everyday 'running' status. Given the abysmal facilities afforded the GE 'outstation shops', a simple organisational

Engine work amongst the usual clutter, 2-4-0 No. 709 on 12th September 1910.

K. Nunn/LCGB

shuffle (with a reduction in staff) was probably all that was necessary. The existing equipment could then be devoted to the routine more in keeping with a simple country engine shed.

It was not long after the Grouping that improvements were considered necessary at Lynn:

'LNER Locomotive Committee 24th March 1927. The Turntable at Kings Lynn is only

45' 7" in diameter and as, owing to its girders being of weak design, the table is under constant strain when the larger locos at present working to Kings Lynn turn upon it, there is considerable risk of breakdown. Moreover, it is not large enough to accommodate engines of the 1,500 class wheelbase 48' 3" and the smaller Atlantic type wheelbase 48' 5" and certain goods engines of similar wheelbase, with the result that such

Claud No. 8890 at King's Lynn in June 1938. Engines backed out from here into the 'Dead End', before proceeding to 'the Passenger'. The turntable remained relatively small and engines larger than a 4–4–0 were seldom, if ever, allocated to the shed. Beyond is the coaling shelter and stack; the work was hard at Lynn, with two men ('and an extra one') to a shift and expected to get through a ten ton truck each. At peak periods enginemen on shed duties frequently gave an unofficial hand. The coal shelter was 'most inadequate', the wind and rain driving in to mix with the swirling dust. Coaling was almost invariably 'from the door', the truck flap simply propped up by a trestle arrangement. The coalmen's hut was particularly unsalubrious, a table and two forms, a single light-bulb and a small coal stove. Later on they managed to get a sink and cold water tap, having previously had only a bucket to 'wash up' in – 'most of the muck went home with them'. The enginemen got a new mess room after the war, when the former air raid shelter was generously given over for their use.

R. F. Roberts

No. 7837 'at the top' of the shed on 29th May 1937. Engines awaiting or under repair were often to be found in this part of the yard though the shear-legs, it would seem, were not used over-frequently.

H. C. Casserley

2–4–0 No. 7418 on 23rd April 1933.

H. F. Wheeller

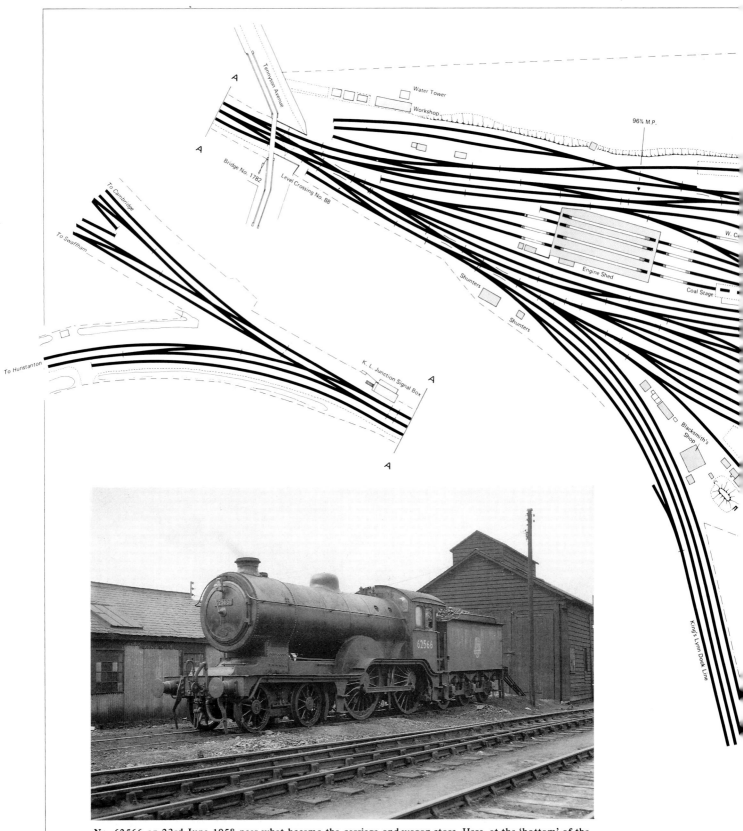

No. 62566 on 23rd June 1958 near what became the carriage and wagon store. Here, at the 'bottom' of the shed, were a number of older buildings, and the site, it is thought, of the original shed. 'A gaggle of huts' hereabouts included the old enginemen's messroom, fitters' and blacksmiths' shops, and if an earlier shed had existed, there was certainly no tradition of it at King's Lynn. Further on, 'dead' engines were often stored in the goods yard itself, either in the 'Fish Siding' or the obscurely named 'Albert'.

K. Cook

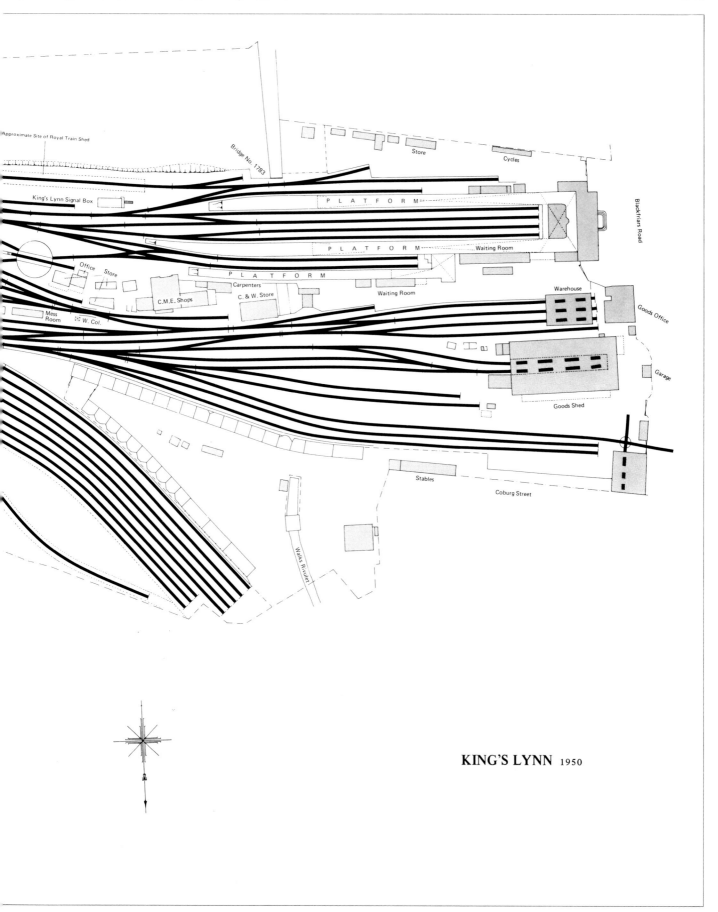

Approximate Site of Royal Train Shed

Bridge No. 1783

Store

Cycles

King's Lynn Signal Box

Blackfriars Road

P L A T F O R M

P L A T F O R M

Waiting Room

Office Store

P L A T F O R M

Carpenters

C. & W. Store

Waiting Room

Warehouse

Goods Office

C.M.E. Shops

Mess Room

W. Col.

Goods Shed

Garage

Stables

Coburg Street

Walks Rivulet

KING'S LYNN 1950

King's Lynn in 1955. It was possible to walk to the shed from here, but access was more normally via a footpath from the station. Running alongside and beyond the shed was the 'Bottom Yard', the 'Top Yard', being at Extons Road over the crossing. The bottom yard had two main arrival or reception roads, the 'Long Siding' and the 'Down Straight'. It was possible for a goods to run in and block the shed, and the yard might ring up for an engine to be moved, if a goods working was early. Lynn was a busy place and in steam days had three pilots at least, and at times up to five. As well as 'Top' and 'Bottom' yards, the 'Harbour Shunt' and 'Dock Shunt' had to be taken care of.

John H. Meredith

King's Lynn with Ivatt moguls, presumably off the M & GN line. *Dr. I. C. Allen*

4—4—0s at 'the top end' in October 1953. Despite its bustling nature and although the ex M & GN South Lynn shed was rebuilt, the GE depot saw no improvements. The 'gaggle of huts' at the 'bottom' were rat-infested for years and when, for some obscure reason, it was decided to have the old gas pipes up, they were found to have vanished through corrosion, leaving only earth tunnels in the ground. Electricity was used only for lighting and all the messrooms had coal stoves for boiling kettles or whatever. Hot water for washing came via a bucket from the nearest engine and the toilets were deeply unattractive. Most men would rather use the station and pay for the privilege. *B. K. B. Green*

Steam was reportedly barred from 12th April 1960, the shed 'to be used exclusively for diesel workings'. Odd locos, however, continued to turn up that summer, and at least one J17 was available in 1960, to aid in the building's demolition. 30th August 1959. *L. Hanson*

engines cannot be used for the ordinary passenger and goods train services or for the royal train to and from Kings Lynn.

'A 50' turntable, which has been recovered from the Berwick Loco depot. recently closed, is now at hand at Doncaster, and it was recommended that it be installed at Kings Lynn in place of the existing table. This would enable engines of the type previously mentioned to work to and from that place. The Berwick turntable would require reconditioning and, owing to its girder diameter, it would be necessary to put it down on a slightly different centre. This would require the demolition of toilets (already complained about) of primitive type to avoid interference with running lines. Approved cost of £963.'

The old Berwick 'table was enlarged, it would seem, for by 1932 the diameter is given as 52 ft. This was quite adequate for 'B12', 'B17', etc. 4-6-0s which appeared on excursions but King's Lynn in the main remained a preserve of the smaller types, 4-4-0s, 2-4-0s and 0-6-0s to the end. Lynn GE men took them to Hunstanton, Wells via Heacham, Dereham and Norwich, Thetford via Swaffham, March via Ely Curve and via Wisbech, and Peterborough via March. Liverpool Street trains were relieved at Ely or Cambridge in these earlier times but later King's Lynn men worked all the way to London.

King's Lynn seems to have 'officially closed' on 12th April 1959, still in the Cambridge District and coded 31C. Diesels and odd steam visitors continued to stable at the shed, intact with all its facilities quite late in the year and continued to do so, quite probably, well into

1960. In that year the shed was at last demolished, pulled down by a 'J17' 0-6-0, armed with a chain from the coupling to the side wall of the shed.

The following allocations indicate Kings Lynn to have been a haven of original GE types throughout LNER times. This situation continued to prevail over some twenty years of BR rule:

1933:

'D13' 4-4-0 Nos. 7708, 7718, 7732, 7742, 8036
'D15' 4-4-0 Nos. 8792, 8797, 8863, 8893
'E4' 2-4-0 Nos. 7418, 7444, 7458, 7462, 7464, 7476, 7477, 7480, 7503
'F3' 2-4-2T Nos. 8061, 8084, 8085, 8091
'J15' 0-6-0 Nos. 7526, 7530, 7627, 7801, 7831, 7840, 7842, 7847, 7869, 7913
'J16' 0-6-0 Nos. 8180, 8185
'J66' 0-6-0T Nos. 7290, 7299
'J67' 0-6-0T Nos. 7199, 7402, 7403
'J68' 0-6-0T Nos. 7308, 7309
'J69' 0-6-0T Nos. 7301

1936:

'D9' 4-4-0 Nos. 5109, 6015, 6018, 6035
'D13' 4-4-0 Nos. 7706, 8029, 8035, 8036, 8039
'D15' 4-4-0 Nos. 7835, 7840, 7869, 7913, 8868, 8893
'D16' 4-4-0 Nos. 8792, 8797
'E4' 2-4-0 Nos. 7441, 7476, 7492, 7502, 7503, 7506, 7698
'F3' 2-4-2T No. 8097
'J15' 0-6-0 No. 7552
'J17' 0-6-0 Nos. 8180, 8185

'J19' 0-6-0 No. 8269
'J66' 0-6-0T Nos. 7275, 7277, 7301, 7319
'J67' 0-6-0T Nos. 7402, 7403
'J69' 0-6-0T Nos. 7271, 7359
'J70' 0-6-0T Nos. 7130, 7137
'Y6' 0-4-0T No. 07125

1950:

'D16' 4-4-0 Nos. 62514, 62516, 62518, 62534, 62559, 62565, 62569, 62573, 62575, 62579, 62582, 62601, 62606, 62614
'J15' 0-6-0 Nos. 65359
'J17' 0-6-0 Nos. 65501, 65518, 65519, 65521, 65526, 65527, 65530, 65544, 65549, 65562, 65568, 65582
'F6' 2-4-2T Nos. 67221, 67227
'C12' 4-4-2T Nos. 67360, 67367, 67374
'J67' etc. 0-6-0T Nos. 68490, 68495, 68498, 68502, 68545, 68635

1954:

'D16' 4-4-0 Nos. 62501, 62502, 62505, 62506, 62507, 62512, 62513, 62514, 62518, 62559, 62569, 62575, 62582, 62601, 62614
'J19' 0-6-0 Nos. 64640, 64642, 64654, 64658, 64672
'J15' 0-6-0 Nos. 65359, 65378, 65437
'J17' 0-6-0 Nos. 65519, 65527, 65530, 65542, 65544, 65548, 65549, 65572
'F6' 2-4-2T Nos. 67221
'Y6' 0-4-0T 'Trams' 68082, 68083
'J70' 0-6-0T 'Trams' 68217, 68222, 68223, 68225
'J67' etc. 0-6-0T Nos. 68490, 68493, 68494, 68502, 68514, 68515, 68545, 68656

Ely in December 1910. Macallan's writings of 1866-1867 reveal nothing of Ely shed — the early building would not have been standing at this time but certainly engines were working from there. It may well have been a 'floating' allocation, drawn from Cambridge's 'eccentric collection of bygones'.
Collection Michael Brooks

ELY

The first engine shed at Ely opened in about 1847, with the beginnings of this busy country junction. This early 'Engine House' was a long single road building located on the siding leading south from the latter day shed. It lay south of the turntable (the siting of which in turn dated from 1847) nearer to Ely Dock Junction, spare ground either side of the track indicating its former position. This shed had a brief life and had disappeared by 5th December 1866: 'Engine Stable Ely. An Engine Shed is required at Ely capable of holding 4 Engines to replace the stable which was there formerly — Engines located at that Station having to stand out of doors during the Winter are liable to have their Feed Pipes frozen up, and the Work should therefore be put in hand at once.' On 2nd January 1867 it was further discussed, in that 'Design No. 1 will cost £2,400, Design No. 2 will cost £1,500'. The latter, of course, was chosen and the result, its cheap construction only too evident, seems to have been erected later in the year. It was an extremely long structure single road like its predecessor but, at over 100 ft, something around double the length. It was a dull building, a mean 'dutch barn' structure of corrugated iron and timber.

The turntable remained at its original size, an increasing inconvenience first brought to attention in 1872. The Way and Works Committee on 13th August examined a request from the Engineer 'for a 45′ Engine Turntable at Ely, to be procured from the Manchester Steel and Railway plant Co. who supplied the last. Last price was £285 ... Agreed.' The latter sentiment was and is, of course, highly flexible

Ely 'from the roof of a carriage', like the view above, taken on 15th December 1910. Part of the Cambridge District in Great Eastern days and a sub-shed of Cambridge under the LNER and British Railways, nevertheless Ely turns could be worked by a variety of engines. This was certainly the case in later times, though the practice, likely enough, had gone on for years. Lynn engines were outbased on occasions and March men and locos did some jobs.
Collection Michael Brooks

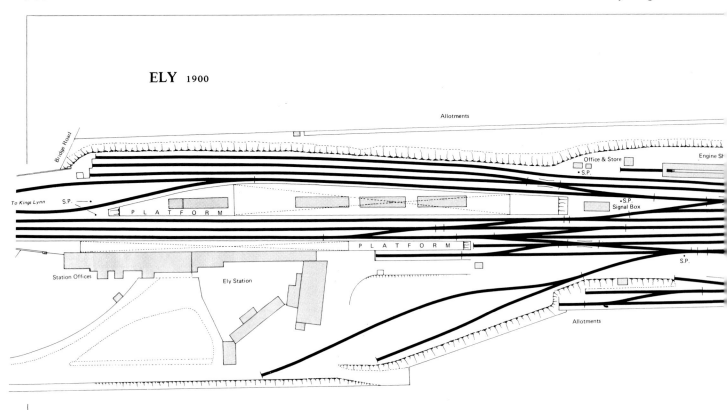

ELY 1900

Southwards, the shed looked onto the Ouse and a siding ran from the shed yard down to the great river's banks, making a connection to Ely Dock.
Collection Michael Brooks

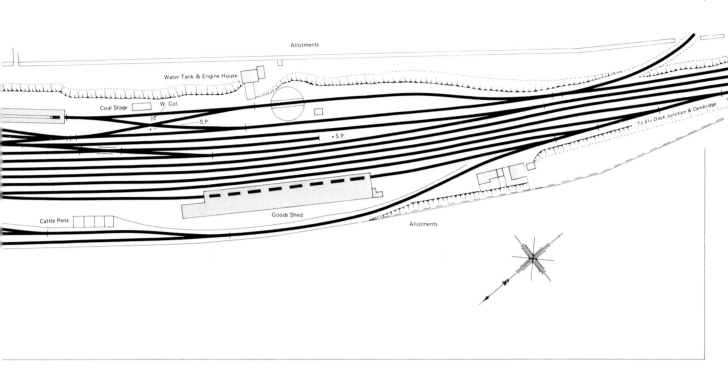

in railway terms and the old 'table had yet some seven years of use, indeed possibly more: '1st July 1879. Engine Turntable at Ely which is about to be removed and replaced by a new one . . . could be placed at Newmarket as it is a more suitable one than the 'table now there. Estimated cost £125.' This marked a considerable rearrangement at Ely and the prominent water tank, which in turn outlived the shed itself, dates from a year or so later. On 20th April 1880 the tender of W. Bell and Sons was accepted for 'the Tank House and Tank, Ely, £648'. 'Acceptance' appears to have been another flexible GER concept for two weeks later on 4th May the project was 'declined due to alterations and fresh tenders invited'. It finally appears to have been built later in the year. The shed eluded a disastrous fire of 6th April 1889, which destroyed 'Goods Shed, Grain Shed and seven buildings at Ely station . . . the origin of which is involved in mystery . . . '

Around 1912 the old turntable of 1879 was in its turn replaced. The new example, much larger, was placed closer to the shed on a separate spur, which took its leave of the original siding approximately at the site of the old turntable, removed with its pit filled in. 18th July 1912: 'The Engine Turntable at this place, 45 feet 3 inches diameter, is almost worn out and it is suggested that a new one be provided, 55 ft in diameter. Cost of turntable pit, engine pit and other work = £1,135, turntable cost = £572.' In May 1930, the LNER Locomotive Committee approved a further £384 for a better water supply at the shed. It had for many years been taken from Cawdle Fen, but the nearby River Ouse was recommended, 'being of better quality'.

Ely was the principal outstation of Cambridge, remaining almost to the end a major

J17 0−6−0 No. 65582 on 19th February 1961. Engines continued to make use of the site after the building had disappeared, coming from March as well as Cambridge; more or less to the end March men took a light engine at about 8.15 a.m. to Ely to work a pick-up goods to St. Ives, locally known as the 'Pork and Lard' branch.   *K. Fairey*

sub-shed. An 0−6−0T was provided almost continuously over the years to shunt this important junction, accompanied by 4−4−0s and 0−6−0s in varying proportions. In 1931 there were no less than three 'Clauds' together with an 'E4' 2−4−0, three 'J15' 0−6−0s and a heavier goods engine, either 'J19' or 'J20'. By 1937 there were half a dozen engines, a pair of 'Claud' 4−4−0s, three 'J15s' (substituted occasionally by 'J17s') and a 'J69' tank. In July

1939 there were only five engines and by 1954 only two or three, 'J15' or 'J17' 0−6−0s.

The crumbling building was removed, through age or accident, at an unknown date, leaving the tall water tank the principal feature at Ely. Locomotives, still 0−6−0s, 'J17s', etc., continued to make use of the site more or less until the end of steam; this presumably came in 1962, with complete dieselisation at Cambridge.

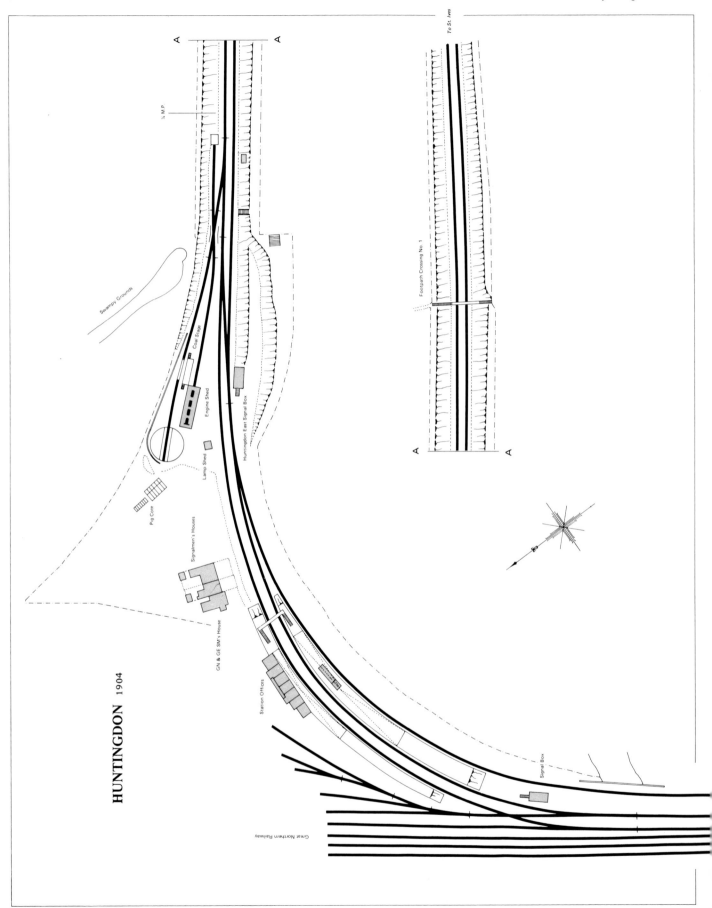

HUNTINGDON 1904

To St. Ives

Footpath Crossing No. 1

A A

¼ M.P

Swampy Grounds

Coal Stage

Engine Shed

Huntingdon East Signal Box

Lamp Shed

Pig Cote

Signalmen's Houses

GN & GE SM's House

Station Offices

Signal Box

Great Northern Railway

Huntingdon shed on 18th May 1937 with a train passing on the Great Northern main line beyond. It was a little known place, home for years to a solitary 2−4−2T; No. 1085 was there in 1920, and also No. 500. From the later part of the 1930s an 0−6−0 J15 could usually be found there and F3s noted included No. 8044 on 2nd September 1933, 8063 on 30th October 1934 and 8061 on 8th June 1938. *W. A. Camwell*

HUNTINGDON

The exact nature of the connections made at Huntingdon between the Great Eastern, the Great Northern and the Midland are both complex and contentious. The original line from St. Ives opened in 1847 to a terminus outside the town (later to become 'Godmanchester'), and a connection (as the East Anglian Railways) to the GNR appears to have been made in 1851, a year after the Great Northern opened its own station. *The Locomotive Magazine* of March 1903 contains a tantalising reference to a train wrongly routed into 'the shed' in 1856, causing severe damage; whatever, a tiny brick engine shed, some 15 ft by 52 ft with coal stage and 50 ft diameter turntable was in existence in 1904. Plans of 1885 reveal an exactly similar track layout but no shed; the coal stage is in the same position and the 'shed' is recorded simply as a siding, ending in a sand drag, or the 1880s equivalent thereof. There was one locomotive in 1885, but no accommodation was available, confirming, indeed, the *Locomotive Magazine's* account of events in the 1850s, in which case Huntingdon shed was re-erected in the latter part of the nineteenth century.

Huntingdon ('East' from 1923, named after the nearby joint station of 1883) remained a tiny outpost of the Cambridge District, by 1917 providing work for only two crews, a driver in charge of one acting driver and two acting firemen. They appear not to have had more than a single locomotive to care for, a 2−4−2T for the local passenger service sufficing over a very long period. An 'F3', changed weekly, was present throughout much of the earlier LNER period but by the late 1930s had given way to a single 'J15' 0−6−0. The shed itself is believed to have finally closed in 1959.

The Great Eastern kept its sheds well provendered, if nothing else. Its generous coal stack was more than enough for the branch tank and was presumably available for visiting locomotives as well. Early locos were a variety of Cambridge stalwarts − Sinclair V 2−4−2WT No. 153 was derailed there on 16th March 1866 and on 5th April W 2−2−2 No. 294 was at work on the 10.10 a.m. Cambridge-Huntingdon. On the same day the 12.5 p.m. goods Huntingdon-Cambridge was double-headed, Vulcan 2−4−0 No. 172 piloting 'Jenny Lind' 2−2−2 No. 107. By late 1887 Johnson T7 0−4−2T No. 85 was on the branch train. *National Railway Museum*

SAFFRON WALDEN

The shed at Saffron Walden seems to have been in operation by 1866, the line had been opened from Audley End the previous year and was completed on to Bartlow 'in October 1866'. Notes exist showing various 2–4–0WTs together with 2–2–2Ts, 2–2–2s and 2–4–0s out-stationed from Cambridge. The GER had resolved to inform the Saffron Walden Company on 30th August 1865 that it would work the line 'at cost price' and in October 1866 the Secretary of the Saffron Walden Railway had written: 'The line to Bartlow opened on the 22nd inst....' The Board of Trade had required them to install 'a suitable turntable at Bartlow ... within 3 months' and a 40 ft 'table was also provided outside the single road shed. For many years, until at least the late 1890s, a carriage shed was also provided close by. On 4th December 1866 it was noted that 'the line must now be considered in Great Eastern hands.

The contractor has discharged his men and the care of the whole line must rest on the Great Eastern Company.'

The little shed was probably at its peak in the 1890s when engines were prepared for a through London service but for the great part of its somnolent existence, it saw little more than the branch tanks, a surprising variety detailed at great length, far more so than could be appropriate here, in a number of GERS *Journal* items and, of course, in the book by Peter Paye (OPC). Ever an outstation of Cambridge, in GE days a driver-in-charge managed daily affairs, the remainder of the depot staff comprising two drivers, two acting drivers, a fireman, four acting firemen and a cleaner. Five footplate crews together with a cleaner made it a centre of some considerable activity despite its tiny size; 2–4–2Ts dominated the work for many years with 'G4'

0–4–4Ts prominent from the 1930s. 'Imports' were later of note – 'C12s' of GNR origin taking over before the Second World War followed by ex-NER 'G5' 0–4–4Ts. In 1937 engines working from the shed included 'F4' 2–4–2T No. 7174 and 'G5' 0–4–4Ts Nos. 8105 and 8139. A pair of 'G5s' sufficed in 1954. From 1939 to 1945 'C12s' Nos. 4509, 4520 and 4534 were the regular branch locos and in the last years 'N7' tanks used the shed.

The shed in BR days was reduced really to little more than a stabling point, the 'table removed in the mid 'fifties and the stage abandoned in favour of a coal wagon simply parked alongside. There was little requirement for the shed after July 1958 when railbuses took over from the tanks though the building was more or less still intact as late as March 1964. It has now been demolished.

The shed at Saffron Walden was an extraordinarily compact place with everything provided for the day to day functioning of the branch locomotives. X class 2–4–0 tank No. 123 was there very early on, in 1866, replaced by goods tank No. 22. The buildings, photographed in this studiedly precise way, have the qualities almost of a model, so neatly are they laid out.   *National Railway Museum*

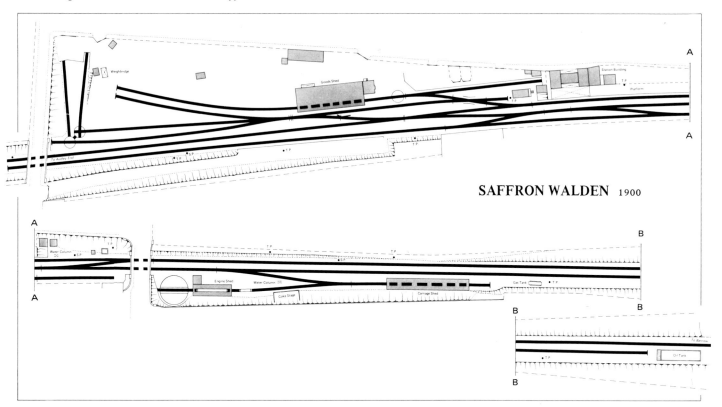

SAFFRON WALDEN 1900

The site at Saffron Walden adjoined a row of solid villas and night work required to be suitably circumspect. The carriage shed was later removed, presumably in response to changing operational practices on the branch and, although the railway was considered a regrettable intrusion, the buildings were at least at one (more or less) with their surrounds. Not so the building which now occupies the site, a coarse and blankly unsympathetic affair more suited to a Second World War airfield.
National Railway Museum

Saffron Walden on 27th March 1937, with 0—4—4T No. 8139 inside. The shed was occupied less than continuously; at times only two engines were at work and they would be out most of the time. A cleaner looked after the engines overnight and attended to any other sundry duties.

W. A. Camwell

There was a quite remarkable variety of locomotives over the years at Saffron Walden, in contrast to many GE lines, worked by an unchanging succession of 2–4–2Ts. 4534 was one of three ex-Great Northern C12 4–4–2Ts working the branch during the war years. *Collection R. Simmonds*

Ex-North Eastern Railway G5 tanks were even used and this line-up appears to represent the entire 1937 allocation, G5 0–4–4Ts Nos. 8105 and 8139 flanking home-grown F4 2–4–2T No. 7174.
W. A. Camwell

7174 again, with 8139 inside the shed on 27th June 1936. The *Railway Observer* of that year: ' . . . Also 7174, 8105/39 are permanently stabled at Saffron Walden, though they appear at Cambridge periodically for repairs and on these occasions are to be seen acting as station pilot.'

H. C. Casserley

The engine shed changed little over the years though the doors, inevitably, did not survive until the end. As Geoffrey Pember writes in a Great Eastern Railway Society *Journal* article, though the chimney suggests a pump, the water came from the town supply. The room below was a sort of office/mess and no doubt allowed a bit of sleep on nights. The chimney presumably served a coal stove, for heating and tea-making purposes.

D. Clayton

Both this photograph and the opposite (lower) example were taken on 4th August 1952. The carriage shed was not even a memory by this time, and the turntable was very largely out of use. It was most inconveniently sited in any case, for the shed could not be used independently of the 'table. It was an arrangement difficult to comprehend, but it was by no means unique (Launceston and Bude on the LSWR alone, come to mind). It was an operational advantage to place the turntable immediately *before* the shed, for then turning could take place independently of whatever might be going on in the building. That is, until it went wrong. The Saffron Walden 'table was taken out in the 1950s by a special gang out of Cambridge which took some days in the task.

D. Clayton

The shed on 28th August 1960. The presence of the diesel shunter is inexplicable except in terms of some special
engineering job.   *John Watling*

NER tank G5 No. 67279 taking coal on 4th August 1952. The stage was abandoned in favour of coaling direct from wagons; it was less laborious
of course, and the gentle pace of life at Saffron Walden allowed coaling to take place at crews' best convenience. 'Big lumps' was the customary
quality; cleaners cleared fireboxes and periodically loaded the debris up for removal. Changing locomotive outlines, presumably, are reflected in
the increased height of the water column.   *D. Clayton*

The station, looking towards Audley End. There was a second water column, on the Bartlow end of the platform, also fed from the shed tank. *Lens of Sutton*

N7s, available in increasing numbers, eventually replaced the old Worsdell NER tanks. Three were sent to Cambridge and ended steam operation on the branch. No. 69692 was one, transferred in 1956 and photographed in August of the following year. The *Railway Magazine* of December 1956: ' . . . following frequent failures of the ex-N.E.R. class 'G5' 0–4–4 tanks, Nos. 67269, 67279 and 67322, on the Saffron Walden branch, clearance tests were carried out at the end of August with a class 'N7' tank, No. 69720. These appear to have been successful, and in the first week in October three 'N7s' fitted for pull-and-push working, Nos. 69651, 69690 and 69692, made redundant from Annesley and Lowestoft were transferred to Cambridge. One of the 'G5s', No. 67269, was later withdrawn from service.' *D. Campbell*

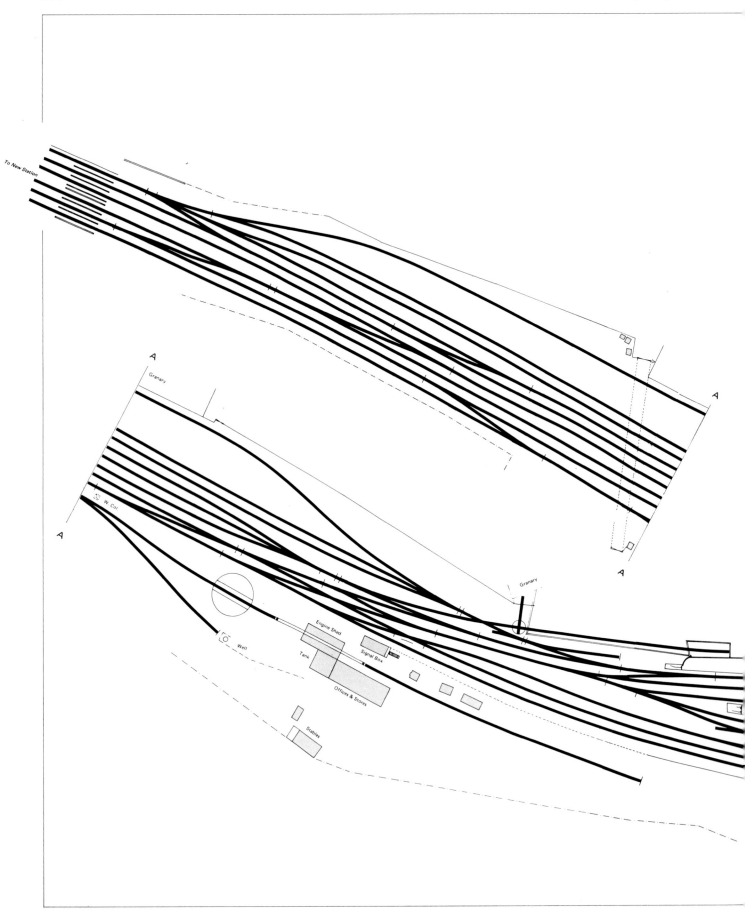

NEWMARKET

The terminus at Newmarket opened in 1848 and plans for the small timber engine shed were drawn up in 1880.

It was a tiny building, dwarfed by the adjacent water tank and set on a lengthy, existing siding. Access for many years was directly from a 45 ft turntable; this remained so until at least the mid-1920s, after which the LNER provided a larger 60 ft example. This had little to do with Newmarket's elderly resident loco but principally catered for GN-type engines on through race specials from King's Cross.

Two crews only were necessary for the single locomotive and it is not known what fate befell them when the engine was withdrawn from Newmarket in the early 1930s. What remained of the crumbling shed was removed but the pit and water tank were retained. Along with the new turntable, they constituted a servicing/turning point, in use for very many more years.

Newmarket on 18th May 1937, the remains of a wholly obscure shed, transformed into a simple peak traffic servicing area. *W. A. Camwell*

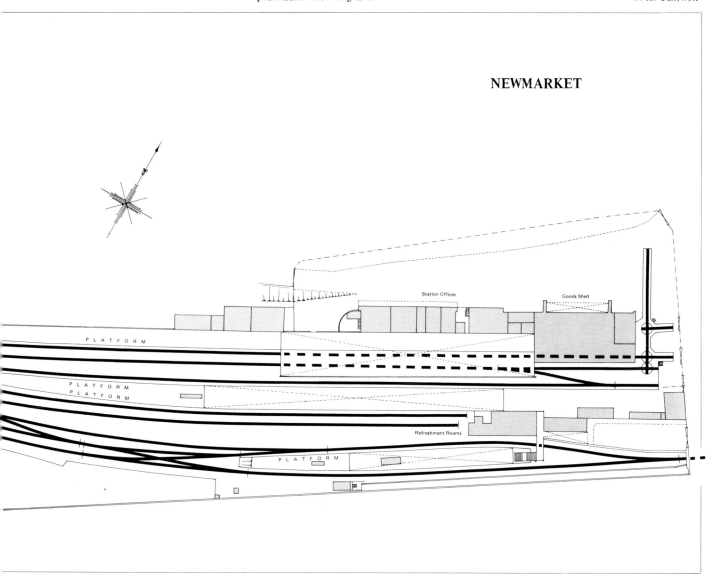

NEWMARKET

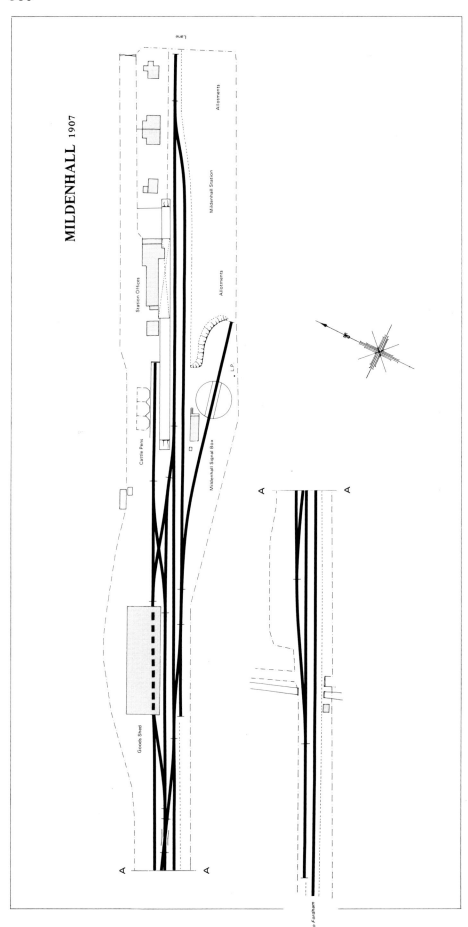

MILDENHALL 1907

MILDENHALL

There was a turntable at Mildenhall, dutifully operated by crews off the branch train over many decades. Services ran some twenty miles from Cambridge through to the terminus and tender locos, 2–4–0s ('E4') and 0–6–0s ('J15') characterised the workings until the end of steam. The station was opened in 1885 with a 50 ft turntable installed from the first. One or two locos were stationed at Mildenhall, in Great Eastern days regarded as an 'outstation', part, of course, of the Cambridge District. There were four footplatemen based there in 1914, a senior driver in charge of an acting driver and two acting firemen. They lived in the town which indicates a nightly/weekend stabling of at least one engine. The practice began in 1885 but homes were not always readily available: '21st July 1903 . . . owing to the scarcity of suitable houses at Mildenhall, 2 cottages are urgently needed for the Driver and Acting Driver stationed there . . . the men are willing to pay 4s. per week, producing a return to the company of 2¼% on outlay.'

Mildenhall was removed from the list of outstations in 1915, an event presumably marking the withdrawal of engines and men. A *Railway Observer* correspondent could note in 1937 that locos 'were at one time stationed at Mildenhall'. Outwardly, of course, little had changed, the habit of using tender locos on the branch remaining until the end of steam – the 'table was still in place at the end of the passenger service in 1962, at much the same time as the withdrawal of steam from Cambridge shed.

Top right: Mildenhall on 14th August 1952. It is an awkward site to classify; the 50 ft turntable represented generous provision but many similar places, busier and of far greater strategic importance, did not figure in the official Running District's listings of 1914. This sort of anomaly is noted in the introduction to Part One and comparisons made with places like Temple Mills and Liverpool Street, both of which could be more sensibly regarded as 'depots'. Anyway this is what the Great Eastern was all about; Mildenhall apparently ceased to be 'an outstation' in 1915 and the 2–4–0s which worked most trains did not even need a 50 ft 'table, or anything like it. It is on record, however, that a B12 4–6–0 did find its way to Mildenhall, working through on a Sunday excursion in 1932, so the 'table was used to full effect at least once.   *D. Clayton*

Right: Railbuses replaced the 2–4–0s and the turntable seems unlikely to have been used after about 1958. By March of that year Nos. 67288 and 67297 had been withdrawn, leaving only 62785 in service, still working the branch: 'On Easter Monday, this veteran was noted hauling passenger trains Fordham to Mildenhall'. The engine was still active later in the year, as a *Railway Magazine* correspondent noted: '. . . on August 27 the new railbus working on the Mildenhall branch developed a serious mechanical fault, and its place was taken by No. 62785, the last remaining class 'E4' 2–4–0. The veteran was still at work on the branch five days later, although it was unable to maintain the accelerated schedules of the railbus.'
                                                 Dr. I. C. Allen

ST. IVES

An engine and crew were customarily out-stationed here, a practice ended in 1922. 'Little Sharpie' 2–4–0 No. 27 had been regularly stationed at St. Ives for the Ely services, locally known as the 'Grunty Fen Express'. Ely shed had traditionally supplied the engine, by the 1920s 2–4–2Ts Nos. 1063 and 1066, provided alternately. No shed building appears on plans, even from the earliest days and it is not known if even a pit was available.

RAMSEY

The town of Ramsey was blessed with two railway termini, each boasting an engine shed. The first, five miles from the Great Northern main line at Holme, was completed in 1863. Its operation was perforce the responsibility of the GN, the Great Eastern majority interest in the capital, however, making it ostensibly the proprietor. Thus was the GE owner of the first Ramsey engine shed, its fate detailed in the following 'Report from the General Manager' of 10th February 1897:

> 'The Directors will be aware that the Holme and Ramsey Railway, which is the property of this Company, has been leased to the Great Northern Company for many years by whom it is worked. At Ramsey there is an Engine Shed built of corrugated iron. It is not required by the Great Northern Company, it is in a very bad state of repair and has been up about 35 years. The Great Northern ask if we have any objection to it being pulled down, its condition being past repair. They assess its value at the present time at £50 which Mr. Wilson says is about what it is worth. The Great Northern agree to that sum being set off against their Capital Expenditure at the termination of the present lease, which will be in 1917 ... Agreed'.

So did the first Ramsey shed, an insignificant and neglected building pass into history. In some arcane regional stratagem of its own the Great Eastern had also backed the independent 'Ramsey and Somersham Junction Railway' which began services in 1889. This junction on the St. Ives-March line meant operations were later under the aegis of the GN and GE Joint Committee. A brick engine shed was erected at this second Ramsey terminus, housing the loco outbased from Cambridge. It was evidently complete by 1887 and opened with the line two years later; a pair of men were based there at first, a total doubled by 1914. The typical complement of four included a driver-in-charge and, at times, a coalman. The passenger service ceased in 1930 and the shed was then abandoned.

Site of the shed at Ramsey, on 18th May 1937. It was reputedly 'dismantled' in 1935.

W. A. Camwell

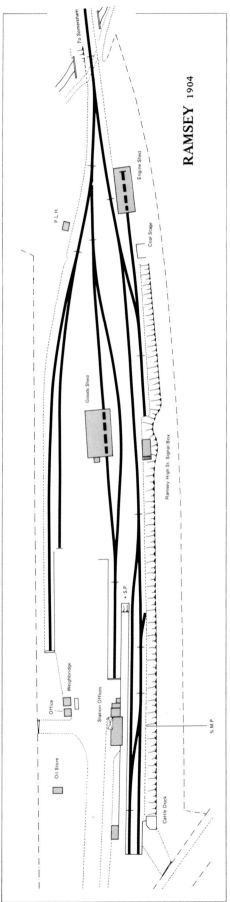

RAMSEY 1904

The train engine at Thaxted, in time-honoured fashion, left its coaches at the station and retired to the engine shed. The Great Eastern should really have known better than to take on the Thaxted line, opened in 1913. Doubtless grants available under the Light Railway Act and free land played a part in the construction of the GE's 'last branch'.
Photomatic

THAXTED

The Elsenham and Thaxted Light Railway was a marvellous if quite absurd venture, though the addition of yet one more burdensome branch line could not noticeably worsen the already shaky finances of the Great Eastern. The terminus sat aloof on a hill distant from the town and over the years the inhabitants were less and less inclined to trek the mile or so between the two.

There was never more than a single 0–6–0T (e.g. 7193 in 1937) based at Thaxted, supplied by Cambridge and exchanged at suitable intervals. Two crews, a driver in charge with an acting driver and two acting firemen, were sufficient for the workings and although 'J15' 0–6–0s are said to have occasionally appeared on goods, no turntable was available. Coaling was from a short, slightly raised siding at the south side of the shed whilst water was obtained through the familiar GE device of a locomotive water-raising cock. (P. Paye, in *The Thaxted Branch* [OPC 1984] describes the work, staff and various incidents at the shed over the years).

The last passenger train ran on 13th September 1952 and with that the shed closed. It remains in excellent condition today, used by a builders' merchant.

There are relatively few views of Thaxted which show people, accounting in part for the line's demise. Thaxted itself lay across the fields and the station can hardly be said to have been conveniently situated. A good coat, boots and cap were obvious precautions when embarking on the trek to the station, in any but the very best weather.
Collection G. Gundry

Final approach was a windy one, up a slope past the engine shed. The branch opened in 1913 a bit late to benefit from agricultural traffic. The pattern of farm products by this time had changed; there were less benefits to be had and farmers had got along without a railway for so long that there was little reason for changing. 27th March 1937.

W. A. Camwell

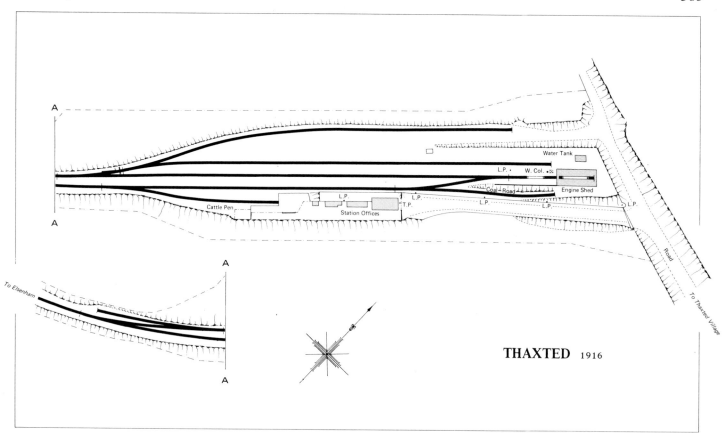

A

A

A

A

To Elsenham

Water Tank

L.P. · W. Col. ·

Coal Road

Engine Shed

Cattle Pen

L.P.

Station Offices

T.P.

L.P.

L.P.

L.P.

Road

To Thaxted Village

THAXTED 1916

Thaxted with the usual GE giant coal stacks.

Collection G. Gundry

Thaxted on 4th August 1952, fields, hedgerows and open sky. Beeching was as yet an unimagined spectre but passenger closure came early to the line and this was the last year of the shed's operation. A marvellously self-contained place, the GER, it seems, was adept at arranging everything in a permanently pre-Great War fashion.

D. Clayton

30th June 1951. The passenger service was worked, it would seem, more or less entirely by 0−6−0Ts; The *Railway Magazine* of 1951: 'The tank engine allocated to the service is normally housed in the small shed at Thaxted, though it forms part of the stock of the Cambridge motive power depot where repairs and major maintenance are carried out.'

H. C. Casserley

The shed was afterwards taken over by a builders merchant but the neglected approach can still recall the windswept, collars-up trek of steam days.

W. T. Stubbs

Stock movement at Hunstanton. Local residents watched with some vigour for any hint of 'dirty smoke' and complained direct to the station master. Tanks were to be found at Hunstanton but were not there continuously; in one four week period in 1936 no tank engines at all were noted, even on August Bank Holiday. Passenger trains were then handled by all manner of tender engines, D9, D13, D15 and D16 4–4–0s, E4 2–4–0s and J15, J19 and J20 0–6–0s, with one B17 4–6–0 on a special. Earliest notes concern a Sinclair Y class, from Lynn, No. 328 and a Johnson 'No. 1', No. 35, on 16th June 1887.

Collection W. A. Camwell

Hunstanton existed essentially to service visiting excursion locos, amounting therefore to quite generous provision, in GE terms. The old shed was single road, with only one engine allocated in 1885, and was rebuilt (unlike, say, Walton, similarly occupied) to overcome the severe operational inconvenience of a restricted site. The new shed opened in 1899 in northlight pattern style (Part One discusses the variations/generations of GE shed building) and, although branch work could easily be handled by one or two locos, on summer Saturdays the place was transformed.

W. A. Camwell

HUNSTANTON

The Lynn and Hunstanton Railway completed its line in October 1862, the services worked from the first by the Great Eastern. It is not known to what extent (if indeed, any) accommodation was made for locomotives in the first years; certainly traffic increased in satisfactory manner and a second engine was soon necessary. The directors heard from the secretary, J. B. Owen, on 30th October 1863: 'the requirements of the traffic render it desirable that a 2nd Engine be on the line and to that end it would be necessary that all the Stations should be supplied with Auxilliary Signals and that two of the intermediate Stations, namely Snettisham and Wolferton, should have proper sidings laid down.'

It was not long before Hunstanton could boast no less than four platforms, the two pairs angled to accommodate a 40 ft turntable, run-round, etc. between the station buildings themselves. For many years the track alongside Platform 2 (the faces were numbered 1-4, east to west) was covered at its northern extremity, an extension of the station building. Attached to this canopy, standing between it and the turntable, was a single road building some 60 ft in length, believed to have been the first engine shed. Water supply at Hunstanton came originally from a well, its 'closure' approved by the GE Locomotive Committee on 5th August 1871. 'The pump and well' required removal to 'another part of the yard. at a cost of about £30, '. . . Mr. Langley, however, suggests that

Train approaching Hunstanton. The 1920 complement was only one engine, a 2—4—2T No. 1062. This engine concerned itself entirely with the branch trains, with visiting locos handling everything else. There was even 'a London' in the 1930s, and it was the job of the Hunstanton night cleaner to refill the restaurant car gas tanks from a flexible hose. A disaster was narrowly avoided when one hapless individual made the classic error of lighting a paraffin flame torch, the better to see what he was doing.

Collection R. Simmonds

the well be closed and we take the supply from the Water Co. . . . We use about 3,000 gallons per week, at a pumping cost of 8/- to 10/- per week.'

With a lively service on the branch, excursions, through connections to London, etc., the inconveniently sited engine facilities became increasingly an operating hindrance. A lengthy strip of spare ground was available to the south, more or less opposite the gas works

and a new shed, in GE turn of the century northlight pattern style, would appear to have opened some time in 1899. The tender for its construction (the 'New Engine Shed Hunstanton' was to hold six engines) was accepted on 7th February that year, an estimate of £1,757 from Kirk Knight & Co. of Sleaford. The shed, laid out in conventional fashion with 50 ft turntable and open wooden coal stage, proved to be generous provision — necessary for

The shed was rearranged from 1937, an LNER scheme reflecting the growth in excursion work at Hunstanton: "The facilities at Hunstanton station are to be improved by the LNER. The scheme provides for the enlargement of the circulating area; a new awning over the concourse, and new platform barriers; a new awning on the east side; and new offices for the stationmaster, ticket collectors and porters. The parcels office is to be considerably extended and platform 3 will be increased in length from 520 to 770 feet; platform 4 will be extended from 515 to 740 feet. Additional accommodation for 43 carriages is to be provided, the engine shed is to be modified to give access at both ends, a new engine pit 60 feet long will be constructed, and further provision made for engines taking water." The coal stage disappeared, new stock roads were put in by the shed and the building made double-ended. The turntable had a revised approach and had earlier itself undergone some considerable refitting. This is presumably the Cambridge crane, on 13th February 1935, with the 'table lifted for examinations. Quite what was found or what the remedy might have been is not clear.

R. H. R. Garraway, courtesy A. Garraway

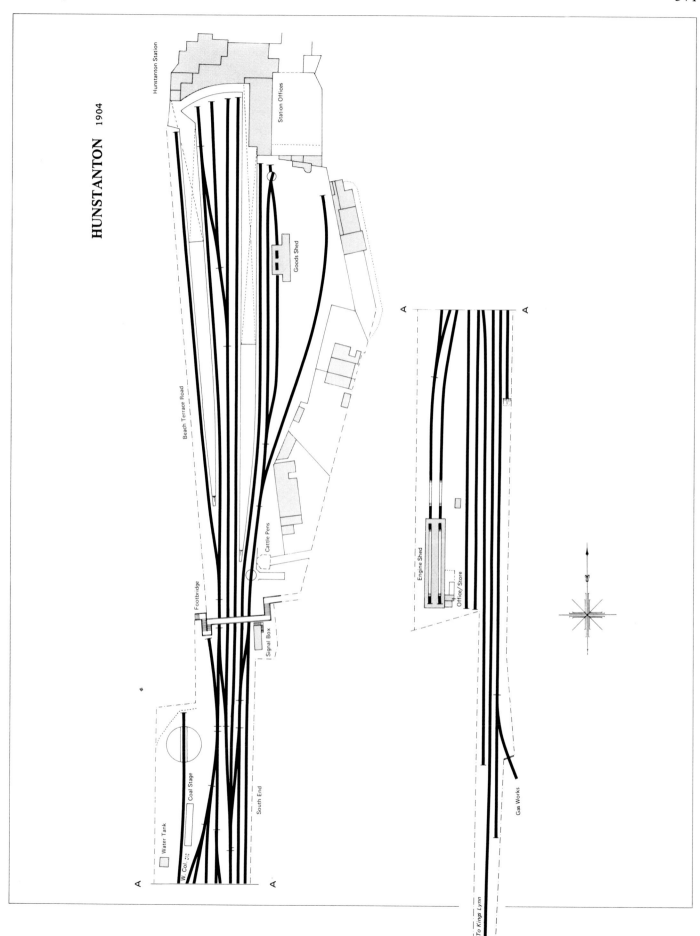

HUNSTANTON 1904

Hunstanton on 1st September 1961. After the Second World War a Claud had been at Hunstanton, a King's Lynn 'Royal' engine outbased on the principle of it being less likely to receive harsh treatment, away from the pell-mell of the main depot. The King's Lynn engine traditionally required two or three days work to bring it up to 'Royal' scratch but the Hunstanton example could more or less be put straight on the job. Hunstanton men were not allowed to work 8783 when it was actually hauling the royal family, a slight which understandably peeved the local lads. They eventually prevailed upon the authorities at Lynn to take 8783 (62614) back. *K. Fairey*

excursion traffic and quite adequate for the latter-day allocation, seldom more than a single loco. 2–4–0s or 2–4–2Ts seem to have been provided until the 1920s but by 1931 a single 'F3' 2–4–2T formed the official Hunstanton complement. By 1939 a pair of these tanks were present, replaced in BR days by 'two D16 4–4–0s'. Whatever the precise variations, it was more or less usual in much of the LNER period to have one 2–4–0 working through the day, double-shifted, and a 2–4–2T ('F3') with one shift only. Hunstanton, an outstation of the Cambridge District, was a sub-shed of King's Lynn, a fact reflected in the post-Nationalisation coding.

The shed was rearranged under proposals of 1937 affecting the whole of the station area, the most notable feature being lengthening of the platforms. A modified approach was made to the yard, involving a new 60 ft engine pit and the shed itself was opened up at the rear, becoming a through building. DMU sets came to the Hunstanton line in 1958 and the shed was reported closed towards the end of that year, in November. Steam locomotives, Ivatt and BR class '4MT' 2–6–0s, however, turned up at least into the summer of 1961, the shed and turntable remaining intact.

Ivatt 4MT moguls were frequently used at Hunstanton in the last years, and an odd feature were B.T.H. Type 1 diesels, not built for passenger work, on summer Saturdays. March-based Brush Type 2s handled excursions, including Sundays, at least into 1962. The site has now been flattened. 29th August 1960. *W. T. Stubbs*

SWAFFHAM

Swaffham was an obscure country shed of most peculiar layout, a two-road building almost at right angles to the running lines with access directly off a 45 ft turntable. An outstation of Norwich, it was closely associated with Dereham and was, latterly at least, almost 'a sub-shed of a sub-shed'.

Swaffham is thought to have opened on completion of the 'Watton & Swaffham' line in 1875; this is, however, presumption. The line joined the 'Lynn and Dereham' which had been in existence since 1847 and it is probable that an engine shed (a turntable at least, to satisfy the Board of Trade) was then found necessary. Whatever, the shed, two roads yet scarcely capable of housing a pair of tank engines, was certainly in operation by 1883. It stood to the east of the station adjoining 'Northwell Pool' which might well have formed the original water supply. Latterly water was purchased, conventionally metered, from the town mains supply.

Swaffham in 1914 could boast a total of four men, all footplate staff. A single locomotive, most likely a 2–4–2T, was customarily provided in LNER days; this warranted little more than a water column, and the shed itself was removed, though its status, however tenuous, was retained, with Swaffham recorded as a sub-shed (1 'E4' or 'J15') into 1954.

In the 1950s Swaffham, nevertheless, belied this 'outpost' status; like many of these country 'sheds', it was a carefully ordered link in the workings of much larger depots. The recollections of Mr. R. C. H. Lock are invaluable here and serve to bring to light some obscure but illuminating details. The GE outstation scheme of things was still at work in many respects through to the end of steam and was far more complex than would appear on first examination. This is likely to have been the case at many of these small sheds – Swaffham's workings were ultimately linked to those of the parent shed, King's Lynn, in almost convoluted fashion. The integration of workings, crews and engines was on a quite sophisticated level far beyond the simple exchange of locos once a week or whatever. Witness the following detailed recollection:

'There were five sets of enginemen throughout the period in question: two sets were Swaffham men, and the other three were supplied by King's Lynn Depot (31C). The Swaffham men were: driver R. Greenwood, passed fireman L. Prior, driver W. Rutland, fireman E. Sutton,

Relief for annual holidays and sickness was supplied by Dereham Depot. Dick Greenwood was the driver-in-charge; this involved filling in timesheets and providing any information requested by the District Motive Power Superintendent at Norwich, for which Dick received an additional weekly remuneration.

The sets worked as follows:

Set 1 (King's Lynn). LE to Swaffham to work 7.40 a.m. to Thetford and return double heading 11.31 a.m. ex Thetford. Relieved at Swaffham.

Set 2 (King's Lynn). Travelled 'on cushions' on 12.45 p.m. King's Lynn to Swaffham, then worked 1.45 p.m. ex Swaffham (double headed) and returned with 3.20 p.m. ex Thetford. Relieved at Swaffham.

Set 3 (King's Lynn). Also travelled 'on cushions' as above to work the other engine on 1.45 p.m. ex Swaffham. Returned from Thetford with the 4.22 p.m. to Swaffham, then either light engine to King's Lynn or attached to 5.30 p.m. goods ex Swaffham to King's Lynn.

Set 4 (Swaffham). Worked Swaffham engine on 6.11 a.m. to Thetford, 7.30 a.m. back, 10.05 a.m. ex Swaffham, and 11.31 a.m. ex-Thetford (double-headed).

Set 5 (Swaffham). Relieved Set 2 above on arrival at Swaffham. Worked remainder of branch passenger trips.

Some of the timings may be slightly out, as this is recounted from memory. The shedman, Mr. Dawson, cleaned the fires, and coaled the engine during the night hours.'

The depot closed with the end of steam, the remaining two drivers transferring to Dereham for DMU work, principally over the Thetford branch. The two firemen transferred to foreign duties, one at least going to New England.

Swaffham engine makes an unwelcome acquaintance with the 'Northwell Pool'.

Collection W. A. Camwell

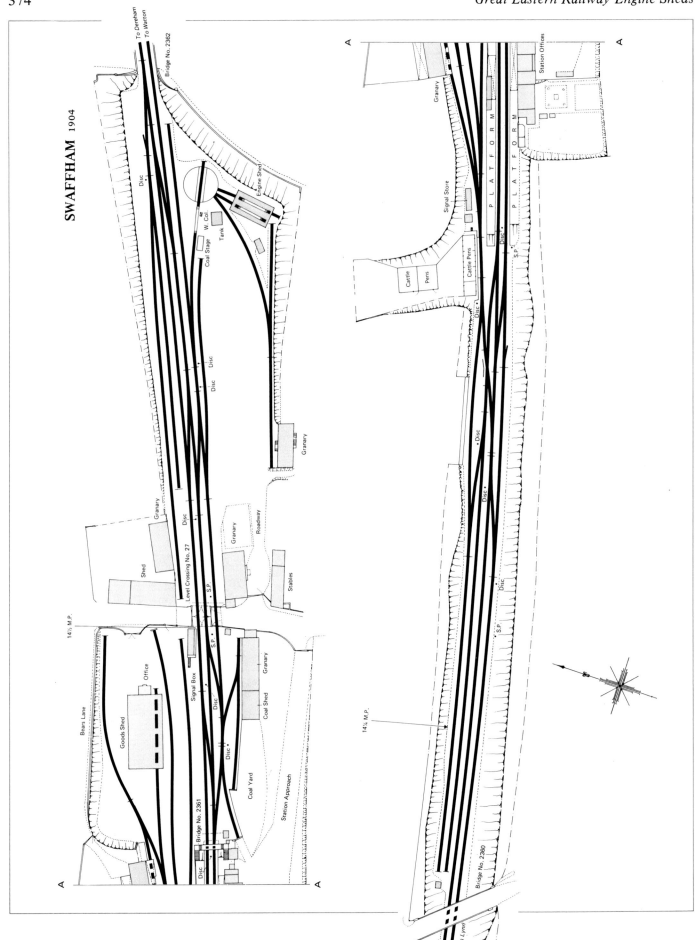

SWAFFHAM 1904

Right: 2—4—2T No. 8085 on 6th August 1939. Engine and crew working at Swaffham was not straightforward and involved men travelling some distance in order to relieve others. The Roudham goods is such a case; it left King's Lynn at 7.15 a.m., followed by two sets of Lynn men. One travelled out on the 9.30 a.m. passenger, relieving Swaffham men, working 'their' Thetford passenger train. 'There was a change of footplates' then the 9.30 a.m. set were relieved by a second Lynn crew which had set out at 12.30. This latter pair worked the Roudham goods back home to Lynn. The process is imperfectly described but the general nature of the work communicates itself. There was also a pick-up, leaving King's Lynn about 10 a.m. and taking some time out to shunt at Swaffham. It was a relatively leisurely task and for that reason was a job for the 'Old Men's Gang', a link comprised mainly of elderly drivers. *W. A. Camwell*

E4 and 4—4—2T No. 67360 at Swaffham. The 'shed man', Mr. Dawson, cleaned the engines and coaled them (from open wagons) at night; day staff saw him only on the odd occasion, his wages being handed over by the early turn station foreman each week. Swaffham closed at the end of steam, the drivers transferring to Dereham and DMU work. Firemen went to other depots, one as far as New England. *Dr. I. C. Allen*

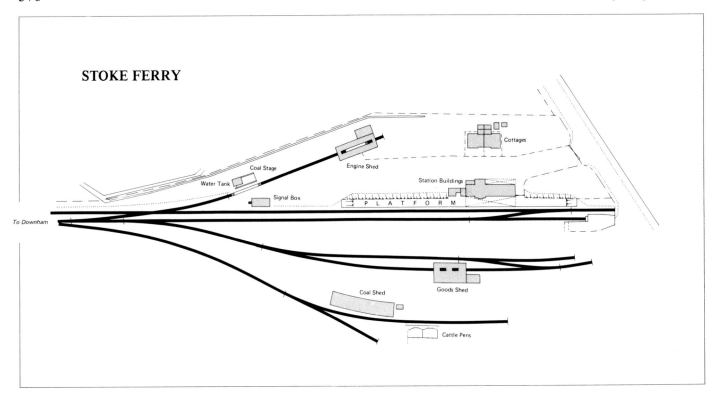

STOKE FERRY

The little shed at Stoke Ferry, brick-built and measuring some 20 ft by 60 ft, opened with the line in the summer of 1882. Very little is known of it, though as an economy measure, the shed closed for a period during the First World War — locos then came directly from Ely or King's Lynn. A single tank engine was sufficient, at one time one of the small 0−6−0Ts mainly intended for the Fenchurch Street-Blackwall service, LNER 'J65'. The shed was part of the Cambridge District with the loco supplied by King's Lynn (some passenger workings at one time extended through to Lynn); there was a driver in charge in GE days, an acting driver and two acting firemen assisting him in the operation of the Stoke Ferry loco. The shed, its removal ordered by the LNER in 1935, closed on abandonment of the passenger service in 1930.

APPENDIX 1
GREAT EASTERN LOCOMOTIVE ALLOCATIONS
Compiled for 1st January 1922

This list is considered correct to a high degree, though oddities remain – engines shown at Broxbourne, for instance, are believed to represent a temporary arrangement, engines stabling there following a restructuring of suburban timetables.

LNER engine classifications have been employed, as elsewhere in the book, with additional labels in the case of the 0–6–0Ts, i.e. sh = shunting, p = passenger. It is only possible in the case of some engines to determine the 'District' allocation and these are noted accordingly.

This listing is available through the labours of others and was painstakingly assembled from primary and secondary sources, including engine records and notes by the late K. A. C. R. Nunn. It principally represents the efforts of A. D. N. Rush and Peter Proud, the results kindly made available by Lyn D. Brooks. It is a long and involved work for which it is difficult to make sufficient thanks. Any inaccuracies the authors reserve as their own responsibility.

BECCLES
E4 2–4–0   445

BISHOPS STORTFORD
E4 2–4–0   464, 478
F3 2–4–2T   1060
J15 0–6–0   846
J67 (p) 0–6–0T   169

BRAINTREE
F3 2–4–2T   1067
F4 2–4–2T   791
F5 2–4–2T   141, 144
J15 0–6–0   559

BRENTWOOD
F4 2–4–2T   577

BROXBOURNE
F4 2–4–2T   171, 220, 679
J15 0–6–0   852

BUNTINGFORD
F4 2–4–2T   106, 235, 582, 586

BURY ST. EDMUNDS
E4 2–4–0   413, 421, 422, 425, 465, 466, 467, 468, 469, 481
J67 (sh) 0–6–0T   13

CAMBRIDGE
B12 4–6–0   1507, 1508*, 1512, 1521, 1522, 1524*, 1527, 1528, 1529
D13 4–4–0   708, 710, 712, 713, 715, 718, 751, 775, 1012, 1021, 1035
D14 4–4–0   1876
D15 4–4–0   1790, 1808, 1810, 1812, 1814, 1816, 1823, 1833, 1835, 1885, 1890, 1891
E4 2–4–0   417, 424, 431, 436, 438, 455, 458, 461, 479, 482, 501, 504
F3 2–4–2T   1044, 1061, 1063
F4 2–4–2T   797, 800
F7 2–4–2T   1302, 1307
G4 0–4–4T   1120*
J15 0–6–0   527, 530, 531, 532, 536, 548, 549, 570, 571, 619, 802, 806, 825, 826, 831, 832, 834, 835, 837, 839, 843, 848, 851, 855, 857, 908, 921, 925, 927, 929, 995
J65 0–6–0T   152
J66 (sh) 0–6–0T   291, 299, 300, 309

J67 (sh) 0–6–0T   11, 199, 397, 398, 399, 402, 403, 405
J69 (p) 0–6–0T   198

COLCHESTER
D13 4–4–0   731, 733, 738, 739, 741, 744, 748
D15 4–4–0   1820, 1882, 1897, 1898
F3 2–4–2T   1046, 1069
F4 2–4–2T   149
E4 2–4–0   498
J14 0–6–0   959, 976, 977, 978
J15 0–6–0   539, 540, 541, 566, 600, 641, 690, 691, 692, 914
J16 0–6–0   1154, 1163, 1164
J19 0–6–0   1148
J66 (sh) 0–6–0T   293
J69 (p) 0–6–0T   364, 384
Y5 0–4–0T   231

CLACTON
D13 4–4–0   734, 735
D15 4–4–0   1842
J67 (sh) 0–6–0T   327

CROMER
D13 4–4–0   1013
E4 2–4–0   440, 441
F3 2–4–2T   1086, 1087

DEREHAM
E4 2–4–0   439, 442, 451
F3 2–4–2T   1047, 1048, 1078, 1099
F4 2–4–2T   666

DONCASTER
D13 4–4–0   704, 1015, 1020, 1028
D15 4–4–0   1811, 1894, 1896

ENFIELD
J68 (p) 0–6–0T   50
J69 (p) 0–6–0T   84, 166, 197, 267, 341, 354, 357, 358, 359, 368, 374, 382, 389, 390
N7 0–6–2T   1000

ELY
D13 4–4–0   700, 1023, 1036
D14 4–4–0   1895
J15 0–6–0   526, 529, 535, 805, 840, 853
J69 (p) 0–6–0T   362

EPPING
F5 2–4–2T   96, 104, 109, 142, 179, 589, 785
F6 2–4–2T   9, 10, 64

EYE
J65 0–6–0T   157

FELIXSTOWE
D15 4–4–0   1822
F3 2–4–2T   1065, 1068, 1076

FRAMLINGHAM
F3 2–4–2T   1066

HADLEIGH
F3 2–4–2T   1064, 1077

HERTFORD
F3 2–4–2T   1080, 1081
F4 2–4–2T   76, 105, 225, 584
J15 0–6–0   511, 870, 884, 903, 909

HUNTINGDON
E4 2–4–0   500
F3 2–4–2T   1062, 1085

ILFORD
F4 2–4–2T   79, 99, 222, 224, 676
J14 0–6–0   980
J15 0–6–0   648, 822, 864, 901
J66 (sh) 0–6–0T   287, 288
J67 (sh) 0–6–0T   14, 19, 203, 257

IPSWICH
B12 4–6–0   1500, 1501, 1502, 1503, 1504, 1505, 1506, 1511, 1515, 1523, 1535, 1536, 1537, 1538, 1539, 1540, 1561, 1562, 1563, 1564
D13 4–4–0   737, 745, 747
D14 4–4–0   1868, 1870, 1871, 1893*
D15 4–4–0   1805, 1806, 1807, 1809, 1813, 1815, 1821, 1839, 1841, 1846, 1874, 1888, 1832
E4 2–4–0   470, 473, 474
F3 2–4–2T   1040, 1041, 1043, 1070, 1071, 1072, 1073
F5 2–4–2T   147
F7 2–4–2T   1305*
J14 0–6–0   984
J15 0–6–0   37, 38, 39, 40, 525, 537, 538, 567, 569, 592, 593, 594, 595, 596, 597, 598, 599, 642, 693, 694, 933, 934, 936, 937, 939
J65 0–6–0T   247
J66 (sh) 0–6–0T   292, 294, 295, 296, 315, 322, 333, 336
J67 (sh) 0–6–0T   16
J69 (p) 0–6–0T   168*, 337*

J70 0–6–0T (Tram)	125, 126, 127, 129, 130, 135, 136, 139	
Y6 0–4–0T (Tram)	134	

KELVEDON

J15 0–6–0	568 (?)
J69 (p) 0–6–0T	194

KING'S LYNN

D13 4–4–0	1018
E4 2–4–0	419, 437, 454, 456, 457, 459, 460, 462, 476, 477, 480, 503, 505, 506
F3 2–4–2T	1082, 1084
J14 0–6–0	970, 973
J15 0–6–0	833, 841, 847, 885
J65 0–6–0T	151
J66 (sh) 0–6–0T	290, 298, 301, 307, 308

LOWESTOFT

D15 4–4–0	1826
E4 2–4–0	429
F3 2–4–2T	1079, 1094, 1095, 1096, 1097, 1098
F4 2–4–2T	654, 678
J15 0–6–0	119, 123, 124, 544, 613, 631, 812
J16 0–6–0	1150, 1165, 1166, 1168
J66 (sh) 0–6–0T	326
Y5 0–4–0T	209

LINCOLN (PYEWIPE)

D13 4–4–0	732, 1025, 1039
J15 0–6–0	520, 522, 528, 618, 897
J17 0–6–0	1173
J19 0–6–0	1269
J66 (sh) 0–6–0T	297

MALDON

F4 2–4–2T	663, 664 (?), 792, 793
F7 2–4–2T	1310

MARCH

D13 4–4–0	717, 742, 1016, 1031
D14 4–4–0	1899
E4 2–4–0	432, 433, 484, 485
J14 0–6–0	993
J15 0–6–0	518, 523, 524, 533, 563, 627, 628, 680, 681, 682, 683, 685, 689, 801, 803, 821, 836, 838, 849, 856, 886, 888, 890, 920, 924
J16 0–6–0	1155, 1156, 1158, 1171, 1172, 1174, 1175, 1176, 1177, 1178, 1180, 1181, 1182, 1183, 1184, 1185, 1186, 1187, 1188, 1189, 1190, 1191, 1192, 1194, 1195, 1196, 1197, 1199, 1200, 1203, 1204, 1205, 1208, 1209
J17 0–6–0	1170, 1193, 1201, 1207, 1218, 1230, 1231, 1232, 1235
J18 0–6–0	1245, 1246, 1248, 1249
J19 0–6–0	1149, 1250, 1252, 1254, 1261, 1262, 1263, 1268
J20 0–6–0	1270, 1271, 1272, 1273, 1274
J66 (sh) 0–6–0T	275, 276, 277, 278, 279, 280, 283, 284, 289, 319
J67 (sh) 0–6–0T	12, 328, 404, 406
J69 (p) 0–6–0T	162

MILLWALL JUNCTION

J65 0–6–0T	153, 155, 156, 158, 246, 249
J69 (p) 0–6–0T	193

MUNDESLEY

F3 2–4–2T	1092

NORWICH

B12 4–6–0	1509, 1510, 1516, 1567, 1568, 1569, 1570
D13 4–4–0	707, 766, 767, 1037
D14 4–4–0	1877, 1886*
D15 4–4–0	1800, 1801, 1802, 1803, 1804, 1825, 1830, 1836, 1843, 1844, 1845, 1863, 1880, 1887
E4 2–4–0	420, 423, 426, 443, 446, 447, 448, 449, 453, 472, 475, 487, 488, 489, 490, 491, 492, 494, 496, 497
F3 2–4–2T	1049, 1088, 1089, 1091
F4 2–4–2T	677
J14 0–6–0	998
J15 0–6–0	120, 121, 122, 542, 543, 562, 564, 565, 609, 610, 611, 612, 615, 616, 617, 629, 630, 632, 633, 634, 637, 638, 807, 808, 809, 810, 811, 813, 814, 815, 816, 817, 818, 820, 824, 828, 829, 830
J16 0–6–0	1153
J65 0–6–0T	154, 159
J66 (sh) 0–6–0T	314, 317, 320, 325
J67 (p) 0–6–0T	161, 164
J69 (p) 0–6–0T	160, 163, 167, 190
Y5 0–4–0T	0228

ONGAR

F5 2–4–2T	94, 782, 784

PALACE GATES

F7 2–4–2T	1303, 1304, 1309
G4 0–4–4T	1110, 1114, 1127, 1132, 1137
J69 (p) 0–6–0T	83, 268, 273, 343, 356

PARKESTON

B12 4–6–0	1517, 1518, 1519, 1565, 1566
D13 4–4–0	756, 765
D14 4–4–0	1869, 1873, 1884
F3 2–4–2T	1042, 1074, 1075
F4 2–4–2T	148
J14 0–6–0	948, 983, 0548
J15 0–6–0	545, 546, 940, 941, 942, 943, 944, 945
J65 0–6–0T	245, 248, 250, 251, 252, 253, 254

PETERBOROUGH

B12 4–6–0	1520*
D13 4–4–0	705, 706, 719, 728, 729, 772, 779, 1029, 1032
D14 4–4–0	1892
D15 4–4–0	1794, 1797, 1824, 1840
E4 2–4–0	430, 434, 435, 483, 486, 499
J14 0–6–0	963
J15 0–6–0	521, 547, 620, 621, 624, 625, 626, 684, 686, 687, 688, 804, 827, 842, 845, 850, 854, 858, 859, 919, 926, 927, 930, 931

J16 0–6–0	1152, 1160, 1161, 1162, 1167, 1202, 1206
J17 0–6–0	1198, 1210, 1211, 1212, 1213, 1214, 1215, 1216, 1217, 1219, 1220, 1221, 1222, 1223, 1224, 1225, 1226, 1227, 1228, 1229, 1233, 1236, 1238, 1239
J18 0–6–0	1241, 1242, 1243, 1244, 1247
J19 0–6–0	1140, 1141, 1142, 1143, 1144, 1145, 1146, 1147, 1251, 1253, 1260
J66 (sh) 0–6–0T	282, 285, 286, 313, 321
J67 (sh) 0–6–0T	400, 401
J68 (sh) 0–6–0T	27, 28, 29, 30
J69 (p) 0–6–0T	191

RAMSEY

F7 2–4–2T	1308

ROMFORD

J15 0–6–0	645

STOWMARKET

J66 (sh) 0–6–0T	323

STOKE FERRY

J65 0–6–0T	150

SOUTHEND

D14 4–4–0	1862, 1864, 1875
D15 4–4–0	1795, 1838, 1849, 1851, 1854, 1857, 1860
E4 2–4–0	414, 415
J15 0–6–0	698, 899, 938

STRATFORD

B12 4–6–0	1513, 1514, 1525, 1526, 1530, 1531, 1532, 1533, 1534, 1541, 1542, 1543, 1544, 1545, 1546, 1547, 1548, 1549, 1550, 1551, 1552, 1533, 1554, 1555, 1556, 1557, 1558, 1559, 1560
D13 4–4–0	1026, 1027, 1030, 1033
D14 4–4–0	1865, 1866, 1867, 1872, 1900
D15 4–4–0	1791, 1792, 1793, 1796, 1798, 1799, 1817, 1818, 1819, 1827, 1828, 1829, 1834, 1847, 1848, 1850, 1852, 1853, 1855, 1856, 1858, 1859, 1861
E4 2–4–0	407, 408, 410, 411, 412, 416, 418, 427
F3 2–4–2T	1083
F4 2–4–2T	71, 72, 73, 74, 75, 77, 80, 92, 93, 97, 98, 101, 102, 107, 111, 140, 172, 173, 174, 175, 176, 177, 178, 180, 181, 182, 183, 184, 185, 186, 187, 189, 211, 212, 213, 214, 215, 216, 218, 219, 221, 223, 232, 233, 234, 236, 237, 238, 239, 240, 241, 242, 243, 244, 572, 573, 574, 575, 576, 578, 579, 580, 581, 585, 587, 588, 591, 650, 651 (?), 652 (?), 653, 655, 656, 657, 658 (?), 659, 660, 661 (?), 662, 665,

F5 2-4-2T 667, 668, 669, 670, 671, 672 (?), 673 (?), 674, 675, 794, 795, 796, 798, 91, 95, 100, 103, 108, 110, 143, 145, 170, 188, 590, 780, 781, 783, 786, 787, 788, 789†, 790†

† error – see note

F6 2-4-2T 1, 2, 3, 4, 5, 6, 7, 8, 61, 62, 63, 65, 66, 67, 68, 69, 70

F7 2-4-2T 1311
G4 0-4-4T 1100, 1101, 1102, 1103, 1104, 1105, 1106, 1107, 1108, 1109, 1111, 1112, 1113, 1115, 1116, 1117, 1118, 1119, 1121, 1122, 1123, 1124, 1125, 1126, 1128, 1129, 1130, 1131, 1133, 1134, 1135, 1136, 1138, 1139

J14 0-6-0 604, 981, 985, 986, 987
J15 0-6-0 507, 508, 509, 510, 512, 513 (?), 514, 515, 516, 517, 519, 534, 550, 551, 552, 553, 554, 555, 556, 557, 558, 560, 561, 622, 623, 640, 643, 644, 646, 647, 649, 695, 696, 697, 699, 823, 844, 860, 861, 862, 863, 865, 866, 867, 868, 869, 871, 872, 873, 874, 875, 876, 877, 878, 879, 880, 881, 882, 883, 887, 889, 891, 892, 893, 894, 895, 896, 898, 900, 902, 904, 905, 906, 907, 910, 912, 913, 915, 916, 917, 918, 922, 923, 932

J16 0-6-0 1151, 1157, 1159, 1179
J17 0-6-0 1234, 1237
J18 0-6-0 1240*
J19 0-6-0 1264, 1265, 1266, 1267
J66 (sh) 0-6-0T 281**, 302, 303, 304, 310, 311, 312, 316, 318, 324

J67 (sh) 0-6-0T 15, 17, 18, 20, 200, 201, 202, 204, 205, 206, 207, 208, 255, 256, 258, 259, 260, 261, 262, 263, 264, 329, 330, 331, 332, 334, 335
J68 (sh) 0-6-0T 21, 22, 23, 24, 25, 26
J68 (p) 0-6-0T 41, 42, 43, 44, 45, 47, 49
J69 (p) 0-6-0T 51, 52, 53, 55, 56, 57, 58, 59, 81, 82, 85, 86, 87, 88, 90, 165, 195, 266, 269, 270, 272, 305, 338, 339, 340, 342, 344, 345, 346, 348, 349, 350, 351, 352, 353, 355, 360, 361, 363, 365, 367, 369, 370, 371, 372, 373, 375, 376, 377, 378, 379, 381, 383, 385, 386, 387, 391, 392, 393, 394, 395, 396

N7 0-6-2T 1001, 1002, 1003, 1004, 1005, 1006, 1007, 1008, 1009, 1010, 1011
Y4 0-4-0T 210**, 226, 227, 228, 229
Y5 0-4-0T 230

'STRATFORD SHOPS'
J92 crane tank B, C, D

SUDBURY
E4 2-4-0 471
F4 2-4-2T 146
J14 0-6-0 951

SWAFFHAM
E4 2-4-0 463
F3 2-4-2T 1045, 1093
F4 2-4-2T 799
F7 2-4-2T 1306

THAXTED
J69 (p) 0-6-0T 196

WELLS
E4 2-4-0 428, 495
J15 0-6-0 614, 639, 819

WALTON
F7 2-4-2T 1300, 1301

WICKFORD
E4 2-4-0 409
J15 0-6-0 911

WISBECH
E4 2-4-0 502
J70 0-6-0T (Tram) 131
Y6 0-4-0T (Tram) 132, 133, 0125, 0126, 0129

WOOD STREET
F4 2-4-2T 78, 217, 583
J68 (p) 0-6-0T 46, 48
J69 (p) 0-6-0T 54, 60, 89, 192, 265, 271, 274, 347, 366, 380, 388

YARMOUTH
D13 4-4-0 730
D14 4-4-0 1878, 1879, 1881
D15 4-4-0 1831, 1837, 1883, 1889
E4 2-4-0 444, 450, 452, 493
F3 2-4-2T 1090
J14 0-6-0 964
J15 0-6-0 635, 636
J16 0-6-0 1169
J70 0-6-0T (Tram) 128, 137, 138

YORK
D13 4-4-0 777

* 'District' allocation
** 'Stratford Shops Shunting'
† Classified F6 in error by LNER, 1923. Reclassified F5 by BR, 1948.

APPENDIX II

ENGINES ALLOCATED AT LOCOMOTIVE DEPOTS
including those in Principal Shops at 1st July 1939

CAMBRIDGE DISTRICT			NORWICH DISTRICT			STRATFORD DISTRICT		
	Cambridge	95		Norwich	102		Stratford	371
	Ely	5		Cromer	5		Brentwood	10
	Huntingdon	1		Dereham	7		Buntingford	3
	Saffron Walden	3		Swaffham	1		Bishops Stortford	7
	Thaxted	1		Wells	4		Canning Town	4
	King's Lynn	30		Wymondham	1		Chelmsford	1
	Hunstanton	2		Lowestoft	21		Devonshire Street	2
	Wisbech	10		Beccles	3		Enfield	14
	March	178		Yarmouth Vauxhall	8		Epping	7
	South Lynn	32		Yarmouth South Town	12		Hertford	8
	Bury	16		Yarmouth Beach	15		Ongar	3
	Sudbury	2		Melton Constable	18		Palace Gates	11
	Haverhill	1		Norwich City	4		Romford	1
		370		Cromer Beach	2		Silvertown	2
				Ipswich	73		Southend	13
				Felixstowe	3		Southminster	2
				Framlingham	1		Spitalfields	4
				Aldeburgh	1		Ware	1
				Stowmarket	1		Wickford	3
				Laxfield	3		Wood Street	16
					285		Colchester	41
							Braintree	3
							Clacton	5
							Kelvedon	1
							Maldon	3
							Walton	2
							Parkeston	32
								570

GRAND TOTAL: 1225 inc. M & GN engines.

APPENDIX III
SOME FURTHER SHEDS

This list is not meant to be comprehensive and other pre-1914 closures doubtless have gone unrecorded. Correspondence on the matter would be welcomed.

BRANDON
Early Norfolk Railway drawings of the 1840s (the line was originally the Norwich and Brandon, opened in the summer of 1845) show a most generous engine shed provision at Brandon. The 'Engine House', a through building, had six roads, each with 'Cinder Pits'. The Eastern Counties took over from 1848 and Brandon's brief career as engine shed was apparently at an end. From *The Locomotive Magazine* of 1901: "At the other end of their system the Norfolk Co. formed a locomotive depot at Brandon, but on the E.C.R. taking the line over, the engines ran through to Norwich, and the loco shops at this station were no longer needed. The building, however, still exists, and at the present time is used as stabling, etc."

BROXBOURNE
A shed was erected here in the first days of the junction for Ware, Hertford, etc, appearing to have been opened with that branch in the 1840s. Broxbourne shed had two roads, one of them with a turntable and, though it closed relatively early in the GE period (the date is unknown), a 'table was maintained for very many years. With its short siding and opportunity for relaxed examination, it proved convenient for engines 'running in' from Stratford. Broxbourne was a standard turn for years and

in the twenties at least most newly overhauled tender engines (tanks went to Enfield) proceeded there at a leisurely pace; 'it was a nice day out' and engines tarried for an hour or two before returning to the works. It made for a break in routine and strange things could happen — fitters travelling on the framing, and on one occasion a 'Claud' fresh from overhaul had, it transpired, been fitted with a coupling rod of less than the desired length. This inevitably ran hot with the further calamity of hot axle bearings, pulled together by the errant rod.

Engines Nos. 171, 220 and 679 are shown at Broxbourne in 1922 but this is believed to have been a temporary arrangement, engines parked following a restructuring of the suburban services in 1920. The practice ceased soon afterwards.

FAKENHAM
The Eastern Counties Railway had maintained a small engine shed and turntable here to serve the terminus. It was apparently closed on extension of the line to Wells in 1857.

MARKS TEY
There is suggestion of a single road shed here 'at right angles to the main line', in use from 1849 to 1865.

SUTTON
There is supposed to have been a one road shed here, presumably dating from the terminus days of 1866. The Board of Trade had required a turntable at Sutton and the MacAllan Dairies

(see under Cambridge) record engines 'sent' there at the time, e.g. 'Jenny Lind' 2–2–2 No. 105 in place of No. 107 in May 1866.

THETFORD
A picture exists of a single road shed here, dated 'pre 1889'. It is of uncertain antecedence and closed at an early date.

WARE
Ware had a busy agriculturally-based goods yard — as early as June 1900 it 'was not big enough' and the 'coal allotments' were to be removed to make way for the burgeoning grain traffic. Horses presumably sufficed in GE days but from 1930 (some accounts have its arrival slightly earlier) a petrol shunter, similar to the Brentwood example and originating from the North British Railway, was put to work. No. 8431 stabled on a short siding in the yard, recalling in principle any number of earlier, genuinely Great Eastern 'outstations'.

WATTON
'The original general offices and locomotive and carriage sheds of the Thetford and Watton Railway' could, according to the *Railway Magazine*, still be seen in 1953. A plan believed to date from Thetford and Watton Railway days, the early 1870s when the station was a terminus, show a single road engine shed with turntable immediately outside. It closed on extension to Swaffham and was soon afterwards removed.

Brandon 1911.   *Collection Michael Brooks*

APPENDIX IV
Sir Vincent Raven's 1923 Report
ORGANISATION OF RUNNING DEPARTMENT
LONDON & NORTH EASTERN RAILWAY

GREAT EASTERN SECTION.

It has been the practice on the Great Eastern section for the Chief Mechanical Engineer, towards the close of each year, to review the position relating to the renewal of Rolling Stock in conjunction with other departmental Officers concerned.

A programme is mutually agreed upon after taking all the factors into consideration, viz:- the amount of money available, the type or class to be renewed, and the capacity of the Shops.

(2c)

The agreed programme showing the estimated cost was then submitted to the Directors (forming the Locomotive Committee) for their sanction, and when same was received, an order was placed by the Chief Mechanical Engineer on the Shops. When rolling stock has been renewed it has been the practice in recent years to replace with vehicles of higher capacity.

LOCOMOTIVES.

The Locomotive Shops at Stratford, which are the principal locomotive works on this section, it is stated, are capable of building 30 engines per annum, and doing 740 repairs, which however does not represent the total repairs undertaken, as in addition to these, the following are carried out at outside places:-

Norwich	120	per annum
Ipswich	130	"
Cambridge	75	"
Peterborough	140	"

The capacity for repairs to locomotives, appears therefore to be 90.2% per annum of the total locomotive stock of the section.

(21)

The works at Stratford, in addition to building the boilers for new engines are capable of turning out 80 new boilers and 120 new fireboxes per annum.

The total staff engaged in the construction and repairing of locomotives is as under:-

	Number of workmen.	Number of Supervisers.	Percentage of Supervisers to workmen.
Stratford	2549	35	1.37
Norwich	112	2	1.25
Ipswich	82	2	2.44
Cambridge	81	2	2.47
Peterborough	59	2	3.39
Total	2883	43	1.49

COACHING STOCK.

The building of coaching stock on the G.E. section is only carried out at Stratford Carriage Works, which are capable of building 50 new vehicles per annum and repairing 4,300, and other repairing centres are situated at Cambridge, Peterborough, Norwich and Ipswich, for which the following staff is required:-

	Number of workmen.	Number of Supervisers.	Percentage of Supervisers to workmen.
Stratford	1551	19	1.22
Cambridge	3	-	-
Peterborough	18	-	-
Norwich	3	-	-
Ipswich	10	-	-
Total	1585	19	1.19

The capacity for repairs to coaching stock is 84.7% of the total stock of the section.

(22)

WAGONS.

The construction and repairing of wagons are undertaken at Stratford Wagon Works (Temple Mills), whilst in addition, a large number of wagon repairs are executed at Peterborough, Cambridge, Norwich and Ipswich.

The Wagon Works at Stratford (Temple Mills) are capable of building 1,000 wagons per annum and repairing 17,000, whilst 10,400, 4,250, 7,900 and 5,700 repairs to wagons are carried out at Peterborough, Cambridge, Norwich and Ipswich respectively per annum.

The capacity for repairs to wagons is 150.3% of the total wagon stock of the section and the staff employed is as follows:-

	Number of workmen.	Number of Supervisers.	Percentage of Superviser to workmen.
Stratford (Temple Mills)	772	10	1.30
Peterborough	65	1	1.52
Cambridge	42	1	2.38
Norwich	99	2	2.02
Ipswich	84	2	2.33
Total	1062	16	1.51

There is an iron foundry at Stratford capable of turning out 100 tons of locomotive, carriage and wagon castings per week.

(23)

Attached are diagrams of the various Locomotive, Carriage & Wagon Works on the G.E. section, also areas of the Shops at the principal Works.

The total number of men, excluding C & W Conciliation Staff, employed on the building and repairing of Rolling Stock on the Great Eastern Section, including Technical & Clerical staff is 5,995.

Appendices A.B1.B.C1.C1.D.D1.

deal with the renewal and repairing of Locomotives, Carriages and Wagons, and building of boilers for 1922, and are considered as fairly normal, as in each case where short time has been worked, the output has been brought up to an ordinary week.

The Great Eastern section Works at Stratford are situated within the London Area and consequently the rates of pay for the workmen are higher than at any other centre.

The Shops cannot be said to be laid out or equipped in accordance with the most modern or economical practice, and there are many alterations which I have no doubt will be undertaken by the Chief Mechanical Engineer, and which will require a certain

(24)

amount of expenditure, and the money for this has no doubt up to the present been difficult to obtain.

I would certainly recommend that the building of stock should not be undertaken at Stratford in the future.

It would however be impossible to close these Works as a repairing centre, and as it is advisable to concentrate all the locomotive and carriage repairs as much as possible, I would suggest that means be taken early to close down the subsidiary workshops which are in no way well equipped, and concentrate all the repairs at Stratford which should be more satisfactory and economical.

So far as wagon repairs are concerned, it is certainly not advisable to concentrate, as these are more economically and satisfactorily dealt with if undertaken at selected points; some of the present centres however such as Peterborough, might be greatly improved.

APPENDIX V

23949

WATER STATIONS, SHEWING

STATIONS.	Waterworks.	Source of Supply.		Remarks.
		Price per 1,000 gallons.	G.E.R.	
Aldeburgh	... ...	... ...	By water raiser from well.	
Aylsbam	... ...	... ...	„ hand pump from well ...	Emergency only.
Barking	... ...	...	10d. a tank.	L.T. & S.R. (seldom used).
Beccles	... ...	... ...	By pump from well.	
Bishopsgate L.L. (Up Suburban Line)	East London	...	6d.	... ... Emergency only.
„ Goods...	„	...	6d.	
Bishop's Stortford... ...	... ...	... ...	By pump from well.	
Blackwall	East London	...	6d.	
Braintree	... ...	... ...	By water raiser from well.	
Brandon	... ...	... ...	„ pump from stream.	
Brentwood	South Essex	...	1/6	„ pump from spring.
Brightlingsea	Brightlingsea Urban Council ..	...	1/-	
Broxbourne...	New River	...	6d.	
Bungay	... ...	... ...	By hand pump from stream...	Emergency only.
Buntingford	... ...	... ...	„ water raiser from well.	
Bury	... ...	... ...	„ pump from well.	
Cambridge	Cambridge University ...	...	9d.	„ „ „ (at Chesterton Junction).	Practically all pumped water now used here.
Canning Town (Victoria Park Locals)	East London	...	6d.	
Cheshunt	Cheshunt	...	1/2	
Chelmsford	... ...	...	...	By pump from well.	
Chingford	East London	...	6d.	
Colchester	Corporation of Colchester	...	4½d.	„ pump from spring.
Clacton	Clacton Urban Council...		2/3 to 1/6	... ... Charges based on scale.
Cromer	... ...	...	...	By pump from well.	
Derby Road	Corporation of Ipswich...		6d.	
Dereham	... ...	...	...	By pump from well.	
Devonshire Street (For Shunting Engines only)	East London	...	6d.	„ hand pump from well ...	Emergency only.
Downham (Up Road) ...	... ...	...	...	
Dovercourt...	Tendring Hundred ...		1/-	
Dunmow	... ...	...	...	„ gravitation from spring.	
Ely	... ...	...	...	„ pump from stream.	
Enfield Town	New River	...	9d.	„ pump from sump.	
Epping	Herts and Essex... ...	...	9d.	„ gravitation from spring.	
Eye	... ...	...	...	„ water raiser from well.	
Fenchurch Street	New River	...	7½d.	
Felixstowe {Town	Felixstowe and Walton Co.	...	1/-	
{Beach	... ...	...	...	„ gravitation from stream.	
Fordham	... ...	...	...	„ pump from well.	
Framlingham	... ...	...	...	„ water raiser from well.	
Goodmayes (Up and Down Marshalling Yards)	South Essex		10d. to 8d.	... ... Charges based on scale.
Gallions	East London	...	6d.	... ... London & India Dock Co.
Greenwich (North) ...	„ „	...	6d.	
Hadleigh	... ...	...	...	By water raiser from stream.	
Hainault	East London	...	6d.	
Haverhill	... ...	...	...	By pump from well.	
Heacham	... ...	...	...	„ hand pump from well ...	Emergency only.
Hertford	... ...	...	...	„ pump from well.	
Hunstanton	Hunstanton	...	1/3	... ... Charges based on scale.
Ilford {Station ...	South Essex ...	...	10d. to 8d.	
{Loco' ...	... ...	...	...	By pump from well.	
Ipswich	Corporation of Ipswich...	...	6d.	„ „ „ ...	Troughs at Halifax Jnc.
Liverpool Street	New River	...	6d.	
Long Melford	... ...	...	...	„ „ „	
Loughton	East London		6d.	... ... For Carriage Washing only.
Lowestoft	Lowestoft	...	1/3	
Lynn	... ...	...	£80 per annum.	By pump.	Payment to Corporation of Lynn for right of pumping.
Lynn Dock...	Lynn	...	7d.	
Maldon	... ...	...	...	„ pump from stream.	
Manningtree	... ...	...	...	„ „ „	
March	Wisbech	...	1/-	„ pump from ballast pit.	
Mark's Tey (Branch Trains only)...	... ...	...	...	„ hand pump from well.	
Millwall (Shed)	East London		6d.	... ... For washing out.
Mundesley	Mundesley	...	1/-	Norfolk & Suffolk Joint Com.
Norwich Thorpe ...	City of Norwich Waterworks Co.	Av. 10d.	By pump from stream	... Charges based on scale.
Norwich Victoria	„ „ ...	„	Av. 10d. /6	... ... „ „ „
Ongar	... ...	...	...	By water raiser from stream.	
Palace Gates	New River	...	7½d.	
Park (Up Goods Road) ...	Tottenham Urban Council	...	1/-	
Parkeston	Tendring Hundred ...	...	1/-	„ pump from stream.	
Pepper Warehouse	East London	...	7½d.	

SOURCE OF SUPPLY, &c.

STATIONS.	Waterworks.	Price per 1,000 gallons.	G.E.R.	Remarks.
			Source of Supply.	
Peterboro'	Peterboro' Corporation	4d.		
Ramsey		...	By pump from well.	
Reedham		...	„ „ stream.	
Rochford		...	„ „ stream.	
Romford (Goods Yard) ...	South Essex	10d. to 8d.	... ...	Charges based on scale.
Saffron Walden	Boro' of Saffron Walden ...	1/2		Discount of 10 per cent. over 50,000 gallons used.
Saxmundham		...	By pump from well.	
Shenfield		...	„ pump from stream.	
Silvertown (Goods)	East London	6d.		
Somersham		...	„ pump from well.	
Southend	Corporation of Southend ...	1/6		
Southminster		...	„ pump from well.	
Spitalfields	East London	6d.		
Stepney	„ „	7½d.		
Stoke Ferry		...	„ water raiser from well.	
Stowmarket		...	„ pump from well.	
Stratford	East London	6d.	„ „	
Stratford Market (Up Main and Goods Yard) ...	„ „	6d.		
St. Margaret's (Siding) ...		...	„ water raiser from well.	
St. Ives		...	„ pump from well.	
Sudbury	Corporation of Sudbury ...	1/- to 9d.		All over 20,000 gals., 9d.
Swaffham	Swaffham	1/6		
Temple Mills (For Shunting Engines)	East London	6d.		
Thames Wharf	„ „	6d.		
Thorpe-le-Soken		...	By pump from stream.	
Tottenham Car. Sdgs. (For Shunting Engines) ...	East London ...	6d.		
Tivetshall		...	„ pump from well	Troughs near Station.
Tufnell Park (Goods) ...	New River	7½d.		
Trowse (For Shunting Engines) ...	City of Norwich Waterworks Co.	10d.		
Victoria Docks	East London	9d.	... ...	London & India Dock Co.
Upwell		...	By pump from well	Emergency only.
Walton	Tendring Hundred ...	2/9 to 1/-	... ...	Charges based on scale.
Watton		...	By pump from well.	
Wells		...	„ „ „	
Whitemoor	Wisbech	1/-	„ pump from ballast pit.	
Whittlesford		...	„ pump from well.	
Wickford		...	„ pump from stream.	
Wisbech Goods Yard & Tramway	Wisbech	1/-		
Witham		...	„ pump from well and spring.	
Wood Street	East London	7½d.		
Woolwich	„ „	6d.		
Wroxham		...	„ pump from well.	
Wymondham		...	„ pump from stream.	
Yarmouth South Town ...	} Great Yarmouth Waterworks Co.	1/3		
„ Vauxhall ...				
„ Fishmarket ...				

G.N. & G.E. Joint Line.

STATIONS.	Waterworks.	Price per 1,000 gallons.	G.E.R.	Remarks.
Blankney	... ...	Proportion of G.N.R. charges.	By pump.	
Doncaster	L. & N.W. Shed	6d.	„ „	
„	G.N.R.	6d. a tender		
Gainsboro'	Gainsboro' Urban Council	6d.	„	
Haxey		Proportion of G.N.R. charges.	„ „	
Huntingdon		10s. for six months.	„ „	
Lincoln		6d.	„ „	
„ Pyewipe Junc. ...		6d. a tender	By pump from ballast pit.	
Ruskington		Proportion of G.N.R. charges.	„ pump. Fosadyke.	
Sleaford		6d.	„ „	
Spalding		1/- a tender	„ „	

N.E. Railway.

| York ... ... | | 6d. a tender | By pump. | |

Midland Railway.

| Kentish Town ... ... | | 8d. a tank, 8d. a tender. | ... | Seldom used. |
| St. Pancras ... ... | | 8d. a tank, 8d. a tender. | | |

L.D. & E.C. Railway.

Langwith Junc.		6d. a tender	By gravitation.	
Markham Junc.		9d.	„ „	
Ollerton		9d.	„ pump from brook.	

G.E.R. Loco' Dept.,
March, 1904.

APPENDIX VI

70586

GREAT EASTERN RAILWAY.

REGULATIONS

AS TO

Seniority, Promotion, Time, Wages, &c., of Engine-Cleaners and Enginemen employed by this Company.

Operative on and from
December 11th, 1915.

Previous Regulations
are hereby cancelled.

Great Eastern Railway.

Regulations as to Seniority, Promotion, Time, Wages, &c., of Engine Cleaners, and Enginemen Employed by this Company.

1. Fifty-four hours shall constitute a week's work for Engine Cleaners, each day to stand by itself. Overtime shall be paid for all time worked over the usual recognised periods comprising a day's, or equivalent, duties at the rate of time-and-a-quarter.

   Time-and-a-half shall be paid for all Sunday duty and be taken from 12.0 midnight on Saturday to 12.0 midnight on Sunday.

   Christmas Day and Good Friday shall be paid for as Sunday duty.

2. Ten hours shall constitute a day's work for Enginemen. Overtime shall be paid for all complete fifteen minutes at the rate of time-and-a-quarter, except in the case of men working a passenger train 250 miles, or a goods or mineral train 150 miles during a turn of duty, when overtime shall be paid at the rate of time-and-a-half. The men's time shall be taken from "signing on" to when they leave their engines, and in the computation of time no short day shall be reckoned with a long one.

   Time-and-a-half shall be paid for Sunday duty, *i.e.*, each hour shall be reckoned as one-and-a-half hours, and be taken from 12.0 midnight on Saturday to 12.0 midnight on Sunday. After the first six hours and forty minutes, overtime shall be paid for all completed ten minutes at the rate of five hours and twenty minutes per day.

   Christmas Day and Good Friday shall be paid for as Sunday duty.

3. As far as practicable, not less than nine hours shall elapse from the finish of one day's work to the commencement of another except in cases of emergency. In the case of Enginemen when work is resumed before the expiration of nine hours, the unexpired portion shall be paid for at the rate of time-and-a-quarter.

4

4. Only services spent in the Locomotive Section of the Chief Traffic Manager's Operating Department as Callers, Engine Cleaners, Acting Firemen, Firemen, Acting Drivers or Drivers, or services spent as Greasers, Coal Labellers or Buffer Cleaners, prior to 31st December, 1915, or services spent in the late Locomotive Running Department shall be recognised when calculating seniority.

5. When boys are taken on in the service and are afterwards transferred to Engine Cleaners, their services prior to attaining 16 years of age is not to count for promotion; 16 years of age being the minimum at which Engine Cleaners are engaged.

6. Men who pass the necessary examinations may be appointed to Acting Firemen as occasion demands, irrespective of seniority, provided they are not under 18 years of age and that they have done at least one year's cleaning.

7. Men of not less than 18 years of age who have done at least one year's cleaning, and who pass the necessary examinations shall be promoted to Firemen by seniority of service counting from the age of 16 years, or when made Engine Cleaners. Should seniority be lost owing to the age limit of 18 years it shall be recovered on promotion to Acting Driver.

8. Men who pass the necessary examinations shall be appointed Acting Drivers by seniority of service as full Firemen, except where a re-adjustment is required to conform with the last paragraph of Clause 7.

9. Men shall be appointed Drivers by seniority of service as Acting Drivers.

10. Clauses 5 to 9 inclusive, refer to promotions within various recognised districts or subdivisions of a district. Each district, or in the case of subdivisions, each subdivision, being treated as complete in itself for this purpose.

    The districts are four in number, and are composed of the following depôts :—

SOUTHERN DISTRICT.

Brentwood	Buntingford	Canning Town
Epping	Enfield	Hertford
Ilford	Millwall	Ongar
Palace Gates	Southend	Southminster
Spitalfields	Stratford	Wickford
Wood Street		

5

WESTERN DISTRICT.

(Subdivision 1.)

Bishop's Stortford	Cambridge	Ely
Huntingdon	Mildenhall	Newmarket
Ramsey	St. Ives	Saffron Walden
Thaxted		

(Subdivision 2.)

Doncaster	Pyewipe	York

(Subdivision 3.)

Peterboro'	Whitemoor	

(Subdivision 4.)

Hunstanton	King's Lynn	Stoke Ferry
Wisbech		

NORTHERN DISTRICT.

Beccles	Cromer	Dereham
Forncett	Foulsham	Lowestoft
Mundesley	Norwich	Sheringham
Swaffham	Wells	Yarmouth

EASTERN DISTRICT.

Aldeburgh	Braintree	Brightlingsea
Bury St. Edmund's	Chelmsford	Clacton
Colchester	Eye	Felixstowe
Framlingham	Hadleigh	Ipswich
Kelvedon	Maldon	Parkeston
Stowmarket	Sudbury	Walton

11. In the case of any fusion of districts, or when men are transferred from one district to another, seniority for next promotion shall rank from when entering the Locomotive Section of the Chief Traffic Manager's Operating Department as Callers, Engine Cleaners, Acting Firemen, Firemen, Acting Drivers, or Drivers. Services spent as Greasers, Coal Labellers, or Buffer Cleaners, prior to 31st December, 1915, or services spent in the late Locomotive Running Department shall also be taken into account when determining seniority. (Service prior to the age of 16 not to count.)

6

12. In the event of its being necessary to move men from one district to another, or from one subdivision of a district to another subdivision in that district, volunteers shall be called for, and should there be no response, the man next due for promotion to those grades immediately inferior to those which it is necessary to fill shall be required to transfer with a consequent advance in pay of at least twelve months with the proviso that:—

    (1) Should these selected men object to move they may be relieved provided that there are men (the option being given in seniority order) junior to them who are able to pass the necessary examinations and willing to be transferred, in which case these junior transferred men will gain seniority and for future promotions be ranked in front of the selected men who object to the transfer and of those men who before the transfer stood between the selected men and themselves.

    (2) Men of such a grade shall be transferred as will allow Clause 11 to be strictly observed.

    (3) In the case of **Acting Firemen** being required, such men shall be transferred as local circumstances justify.

    (4) In the event of there being no men of the next but one inferior grade available for transferring, then the junior men of the next grade to that which it is required to fill, provided they are able to pass the necessary examinations, or failing that, the junior men of the same grade shall be required to transfer.

13. When men are required to move from one depôt in a district or subdivision of a district to another depôt in the same district or subdivision of a district, volunteers shall be called for and should there be no response, the men next due for promotion to those grades which it is necessary to fill shall be required to transfer, with the proviso that should these selected men object to move they may be relieved provided that there are men (the option being given in seniority order), junior to them who are able to pass the necessary examinations and are willing to be transferred, in which cases these junior transferred men will gain seniority, and for future promotions be ranked in front of the selected men who object to the transfer and of those men who before the transfer stood between the selected men and themselves. In the case of **Acting Firemen** being required, such men shall be transferred as local circumstances justify.

In the event of there being no volunteers amongst the men rated at 7/- per day for work usually performed by a man rated at 7/6 per day, then the man to whom the work is ultimately allocated shall receive 7/6 per day.

7

14. Men are not to be temporarily transferred for a period exceeding three years.

When men stationed in the Southern District are temporarily transferred (*i.e.*, for a period not exceeding three years), from a London rated depôt to a Country rated depôt they shall receive the London rate.

15. Men failing to pass their examinations (medical excepted) shall be put back for a period of at least six months before being considered eligible for further examination.

16. Men losing seniority and promotion through illness or accident shall, provided they pass the necessary examinations, regain their seniority and promotion within two weeks after their return to work. This Clause is to operate from July 1st, 1915.

17. Seniority shall be adjusted and future promotion of men shall take place as if the rule set forth in Clause 16 had been in operation since the 1st of January, 1910.

18. In the case of a man being transferred from one district to another for his health's sake, or for that of his wife, or other member of his family, vouched for by medical opinion, or for other *bona fide* family reasons his seniority shall be calculated as set forth in Clause 11.

19. Men serving on Public Bodies, who in the normal course would be required to move to another depôt shall, if they so desire, be relieved from moving without loss of seniority.

20. Certificates will be granted to **Firemen** properly qualified to act as **Drivers** as occasion requires. The certificates will in future be given into the custody of the qualified men.

21. The subject matter in this circular refers, with the exception of Clauses 16 and 17, to future promotions and seniority in connection therewith as vacancies occur, and is not retrospective.

8

22. Wages:

ENGINE CLEANERS.

Age last Birthday.		London. Per day. s. d.	Country. Per day. s. d.
Grade 1.	16	2 2	2 0
	17	2 4	2 2
	18	2 6	2 4
	19	2 8	2 6
	20	2 10	2 8
	21	3 0	2 10
Grade 2.	When cleaning and firing for a turn of duty	3 9	3 3
	When firing for a complete turn of duty	4 0§	3 6§

§ In cases where **Acting Firemen** are taken off cleaning work and perform firing to another man for his full turn of duty they shall be paid as when firing for a complete turn of duty for the whole time made, both cleaning and firing.

FIREMEN.

			London. Per day. s. d.	Country. Per day. s. d.
Grade 3.	1st year	.. ..	4 0	3 6
Grade 4.	2nd year	.. ..	4 3	3 9
Grade 5.	3rd year	.. ..	4 6	4 3
Grade 6.	4th year	.. ..	4 9	4 6
Grade 7.	6th year	.. ..	5 0	—
Grade 8.	When certified to act as **Driver**		5 0*	4 6†
	When driving for any period during a turn of duty		5 6	5 6
	When turning	.. ..	5 6	5 0

* 5s. 6d., † 5s. 0d.—During the period of Government control.

DRIVERS.

			London. Per day. s. d.	Country. Per day. s. d.
Grade 9.	1st year	.. ..	5 6	5 6
Grade 10.	2nd year	.. ..	6 0	6 9
Grade 11.	5th year when working services of less than 21 train miles per day		6 6	—
Grade 12.	3rd year provided they are working services of not less than 21 train miles per day		7 0	7 0
Grade 13.	After having been rated at 7s. for three years	..	7 6	—

9

The **London** rate of pay applies to the following depôts :—

    Brentwood, Canning Town, Epping, Enfield, Ilford, Millwall, Palace Gates, Southend, Spitalfields, Stratford and Wood St.

Except in cases of disability, misdemeanour, or the special circumstances set forth in Clause 30, men who have once been appointed to any of the above rates shall not receive less, although they may be employed on inferior work.

This does not apply to men rated at less than 7s. per day who temporarily receive that rate or over for working a service of 21 train miles per day.

Men who would be entitled to 7s. per day, provided they work 21 train miles continuously throughout the year, shall be paid at the rate of 7s. on those days when they actually work 21 train miles. Any mileage totalling 19 to 21 train miles inclusive to be reckoned as 21 for this purpose.

Firemen working an engine 225 miles or over during one turn of duty with a main line passenger train, shall receive sixpence in addition to the above rates. This does not apply to work for which trip rates are paid.

23. **TRIPS.**

A special trip rate of a day-and-a-half shall be paid to **Enginemen** performing the following work, and for any work where at least 230 passenger train miles are run on one turn of duty :—

    London and Cromer (Double trip)
    London and Lowestoft (Double trip)
    London and Norwich (Double trip)
    London and Yarmouth (Double trip)
    York and March (Double trip)
    Ipswich to Norwich, via London and Cromer
    Norwich to Ipswich, via Cromer and London
    Norwich to Parkeston, via Lincoln.

In the compilation of this mileage, ordinary passenger, special passenger, assisting passenger, attached (passenger or otherwise), carriage train or light engine miles shall all count.

In the absence of relief being provided for Stratford **Enginemen** on arrival at Liverpool Street after performing work that is paid for at trip rate, they shall, in addition to the trip rate, be paid for the time they are engaged in working their engines to the shed for any other work they may be called upon to do, at the ordinary rate for any such time under ten hours from signing on duty, and at overtime rate for any such time beyond ten hours from signing on duty.

10

A special trip rate of a day-and-three-eighths shall be paid to Enginemen performing the following goods working :—

Whitemoor and Langwith (Double trip)
Whitemoor and Doncaster (Double trip)
March and London or Temple Mills (Double trip)
Whitemoor and Parkeston (Double trip)
Norwich and Peterborough (Double trip)
London and Doncaster (Single trip)
Norwich and Doncaster (Single trip)

If men are on duty such a time that payment by the hour would be in excess of the special trip allowance, then payment shall be made by the hour.

24. Thirty minutes shall be allowed for preparing, and thirty minutes for disposing of engines, except in the case of the disposal of tank engines at Stratford Main and in the preparation and disposal of 1500 class engines throughout the system, where 45 minutes shall be allowed.

25. As far as possible endeavours will be made for each man to make at least six days per week.

26. Engine Cleaners' expenses when working and lodging away from home are 1s. 0d. per day and 1s. 0d. per night.

Acting Firemen when lodging away from home shall be paid expenses at the same rate as **Enginemen.**

Enginemen when required to take rest away from home station shall be allowed 2s. 6d. expenses. An additional 1s. 3d. shall be allowed for each completed period of five hours above ten.

Any time fourteen to fifteen hours inclusive to be reckoned as fifteen hours and any time nineteen to twenty hours inclusive to be reckoned as twenty hours.

In the event of men using the dormitory at Stratford the sum of 1s. 3d. will be deducted from these expenses.

27. Drivers, Acting Drivers, and Firemen shall be supplied with an overcoat every year, and **Acting Firemen** with one every two years. The old coats to be retained by the men after they have been in use the specified time.

A supply of short coats, to be used temporarily, will be kept for the use of **Acting Firemen** when fire-lighting.

11

28. Holidays with pay :—

If six months and less than five years service   3 days per annum.
If five years' service and over   ..   ..   4 days per annum.

Acting Firemen shall be paid for their annual holidays at the rate at which they are paid when firing for a complete turn of duty, viz : **London** 4s. per day, **Country** 3s. 6d. per day.

Acting Drivers shall be paid for their holidays at driving rate.

Payment in lieu thereof shall be allowed in cases where holidays cannot be granted.

29. G.E. free passes allowed :—

If over six months and less than
five years' service   ..   ..   Two, one of which may include wife, and children under fifteen years of age.

If five years' service and over   Two, both of which may include wife, and children under fifteen years of age.

30. In the event of its being necessary to promote men to positions that would otherwise have been filled by men who have joined the British Forces and that at the conclusion of the War there is not sufficient work for all in their respective grades, these promoted men or as many as necessary must give way and perhaps go back in favour of those returning from the Navy or Army.

Wm. C. MAY,

Chief Traffic Manager.

F. V. RUSSELL,

Superintendent of Operation.

May 1st, 1916

ACKNOWLEDGEMENTS

Acknowledgements, as noted in Part One, whilst a pleasure, are difficult in the extreme to express adequately, so much is owed to the detailed notes, studies and considered opinions of others. Staff at British Rail offices from London, throughout East Anglia and elsewhere, provided help and encouragement far beyond what might be termed 'public relations'; the staff and resource cuts noted in Part One are as severe as ever and in the circumstances the freely given help and interest of 'GE' section staff is appreciated all the more.

Much of the account would not have been possible without the help of R. H. N. Hardy; his affection for the 'GE' hopefully conveys itself as much in this account as through his own published work. Dr. I. C. Allen combined a unique collection of photographs with fascinating recollection and a most generous hospitality. Canon Charles Bayes was able to comment on many aspects in remarkable detail both from his own notes and those of George Macallan, preserved by him. Peter Proud also spent much of his time in gentle correction and the book owes much to his constant interest and attention. Once again the photographic content has been much enhanced by material from the collection of Michael Brooks; without his help a comprehensive coverage would not have proved possible. Dick Riley provided all manner of help with customary good grace and to him special thanks are due.

R. C. H. Lock gave some most helpful notes, Peter Paye commented to great purpose on much of the text and special thanks are also due to Bob Clow, John Watling, H. N. James, W. Scutcher, A. Foster and Brian Hilton. H. C. Casserley was inevitably able to provide photographs of great interest whilst Allan Garraway is thanked for making available some quite unique work of his late father, R. H. R. Garraway. He also made some most cogent comments upon the text. W. A. Camwell is responsible for some studies of unique quality, and Derek Clayton has again provided material of an outstanding nature. Together with Derek it is appropriate to thank Reg Randell for singular and much appreciated advice and encouragement.

Others who gave their help over many years include W. Potter, W. T. Stubbs, B. K. B. Green, Ken Fairey, K. Cook, J. E. Kite, P. W. Swinger, J. H. Meredith, G. Gundry, L. Hanson, Roger Griffiths, R. F. Roberts, T. J. Edgington, W. G. Rear, Roger Simmonds, Harry Ellis, Charles Goodwin, Ron Fareham, H. F. Wheeller, Roger Carpenter and Geoffrey Pember. John Davies is thanked in particular for the loan of items belonging to his late father.

Some special mention is also due to John Hooper, *et famille*, in the northern link; Jim Rose and Peter Worsley as long as the nice comments continue; Paul and June for constant attention, and Beverly and Wendy who will probably never get used to it.